Adventure Unlimited

Russell C. Thomas

Pacific Press Publishing Association
Boise, Idaho
Oshawa, Ontario, Canada

Library of Congress Catalog Card Number: 88-61305

ISBN 0-8163-0794-6

88 89 90 91 92 ● 5 4 3 2 1

Contents

Getting Started Can Be Half the Fun

Literature evangelist Kenneth Jenkins didn't have to worry about what to say in order to get in the door. He drove his car into a farmyard, parked it, and started for the farm house when he saw a huge Holstein bull grazing in the yard. The bull looked up, startled. It snorted, bellowed, and started for Kenneth, who is six feet two inches tall and weighs nearly 300 pounds.

Holding tight to his briefcase, Kenneth started back toward his car but couldn't get in quickly enough. He hadn't run much since his football days, but he headed for the house. He hoped that after one circle around the house he could jump up onto the porch, but the bull was too close behind. The second time around he succeeded in landing on the porch with such effect that he crashed through a floorboard. The lady of the house by this time had opened the front door and in he ducked, expecting that the bull would follow. The huge animal meekly stopped at the porch, however.

The lady said to her little daughter, "Darling, please go put the bull back in the barnyard." The child went out, picked up a little switch, and drove the hulking creature back where he belonged and shut the gate. The lady must have been properly impressed by Kenneth's unusual introduction, for she readily bought a set of books for her little girl.

Not only do pursuing bulls help literature evangelists get in the door; angry dogs can cooperate too. A timid and frightened literature evangelist found himself face to face with a snarling dog. With commendable presence of mind he jammed his book in the dog's mouth. Apparently thinking it was a game, the dog raced to his startled mistress with the book. She tied up the dog and invited the literature evangelist in.

"Surely God helped you," she said. "That dog is mean!" She listened to the presentation and readily purchased the book that her dog had already delivered to her.

One literature evangelist chanced to meet a beautiful young lady at the door. His training course had taught him the proper words to say at first, "I am engaged in Christian work...." But somehow the sight of that lovely face unnerved him. All he could think to say was, "I am engaged..." Then, embarrassed, he started over again, "I am engaged..." After the third time, she broke the ice by exclaiming, "Congratulations!" A hearty laugh relaxed the tension, and she invited him in.

Impressed to Do the Most Unusual Things!

A literature evangelist always prays that the Lord will direct him as he goes up to the door—a prayer that the Lord graciously answers. But the way He answers the prayer may not always be what the literature evangelist would normally choose. Literature evangelists are also sometimes impressed by the Lord to try unusual ways to get into a difficult house.

Wilson and John were working together in Kisii, East Africa. They came to the gate of what was obviously a wealthy person's home, complete with a guard and a watch-dog. The dog looked mean, and the guard rudely turned them away.

Literature evangelists in Africa are trained, however, to go to every house. "We must come back later," Wilson said. As they walked around the side of the yard, they saw a hole under the wall. John proposed that they squeeze themselves through, and trust the Lord to send an angel to divert the dog's attention. After wriggling through the hole, they stood up to brush themselves off, and the lady of the house saw them. She invited them in the back door. The wife of the local judge, she readily bought the books, studied them, and in time became a baptized Seventh-day Adventist.

Another literature evangelist in the same area suffered an incredible indignity. A Muslim lady of the house doused him with the contents of a chamber-pot. That would seem to be enough to dampen the spirits of any ordinary literature evangelist. But not this brother's. He went around to the back door to try again, pretending that he thought it was another house.

Of course, the same lady appeared; but undaunted, the literature evangelist said, "Lady, I hope you don't treat me like that other lady over there did!" After an awkward silence, she laughed, and incredibly he found it possible to laugh also. She brought him a large Turkish towel and helped him clean himself up as best he could. Then she bought a health book.

Weeks later he called again and made friends with her husband. This time the couple bought religious books, and today twelve members of that family are Seventh-day Adventist Christians.

When Prayers Are Answered Before You Start

Sue Young, in Korea, was seated on a bus with her books, headed for a new village. Soon the bus became crowded, and she felt sorry for a grandmother standing with a baby on her back. Graciously Sue stood all the long way while the grandmother occupied her seat. When she finally arrived at the village, Sue was almost too tired to start her work.

During her first full day, she was arrested and taken to the police station. Officers led the frightened girl right into the office of the chief, who asked her many questions.

"There's going to be a meeting of the village leaders here in about half an hour," he said. "I want you to stay and talk with them." She was frightened and begged him to release her, but he refused.

Soon the leaders started filing in. She tried to leave but the chief insisted that she sit near his desk. The room filled, and the chief stood and introduced Sue as a young girl from the Seventh-day Adventist Church. "And now she is going to tell you what she believes," he said.

"What a thrill!" she later said. "The angels and the Spirit of God took over and spoke through me." She told of our beliefs and then demonstrated her books.

The chief volunteered to buy, but had no money with him. Turning to the head of the brewer's association, he said, "Tu Han, lend me the money." The brewer peeled off several notes from a big roll of cash. Then the superintendent of schools said he would buy, and also asked the brewer for a loan. Several others used the brewer as their banker until his face got more and more pinched, the bankroll smaller, and Sue's briefcase was empty. Then they said, "Don't miss any of our offices. We will see you when you come!"

The chief said, "Yesterday when you got up and gave your seat to that little grandmother, I was sitting directly behind you but without my uniform. Because you were so kind to her, I have been kind to you."

An intoxicated man in Rwanda told one literature evangelist, "Get out of my house." Picking up a chair, the crazed man yelled, "Get out or I'll break this over your head!"

The literature evangelist headed quickly for the door,

pulling it shut behind him. Instantly the chair crashed against the door. He quietly tucked a small book under the door and left. Next day in the market, however, the man saw the literature evangelist, apologized for the way he had treated him, and paid for the book.

Not all introductions turn out to be as thrilling as these, but one thing the consecrated literature evangelist can always bank on: The Lord will never forget that He is sending you as His messenger to that door. He has said, "Go ye," and He has promised, "Lo, I am with you alway."

"To everyone who offers himself to the Lord for service, withholding nothing, is given power for the attainment of measureless results" (*Testimonies for the Church*, vol. 7, p. 30).

You'd Never Dream
It Could Happen!

Fermin Quiliche was faithfully going house to house in Peru with *The Great Controversy*. All during the first day, no one bought a single book. When he passed the home of the priest, he thought, "Why not visit him? My situation couldn't be worse!"

When the priest answered his knock, he said, "You're an Adventist literature evangelist, right?" Then he invited Fermin in and spent some time telling him how bad the Adventist church is. Fermin listened quietly, making no reply. When there came a lull, he brought out *The Great Controversy* and explained it. The great book impressed the priest, especially the chapter on the judgment. He ordered a copy.

The literature evangelist's courage began to revive a bit. "Can you give me a recommendation to the leading people of the town?" he asked.

The priest thought a moment. "No, let's do something else. Come tomorrow at 8 o'clock and I will go with you to see them."

The next morning the people saw the priest and the literature evangelist going together to the government officer. When Fermin began to demonstrate the book, the priest grabbed it and explained it, emphasizing the chapter on the judgment. Another sale.

All morning the priest and the literature evangelist worked together, the priest talking, the literature evangelist writing orders and receipts. All told, the priest sold 22 copies for him.

Charismatic Catholics in California have also sold books for a literature evangelist. Olimpo Lozano received an inquiry from a young girl whose mother was a prayer-group leader. After several attempts, he was given permission to show them a motion picture about the Virgin Mary. A priest and a nun were among the group of 50. To his surprise, some children brought with them their well-worn copies of *The Bible Story*. (He learned later that they were using them as textbooks for Bible lessons.)

The girl's mother arranged for a Bible study following a film every Thursday evening. The meetings were announced in the Catholic church bulletin, and 1,000 fliers were distributed in the neighborhood.

Olimpo visited them in their homes, and many bought books. "These charismatic Catholics," he says, "were like dry sponges soaking up spiritual knowledge. They told me that their previous teachers were all words and no action."

Olimpo's quiet, earnest prayers won the hearts of these people. It contrasted with the shouting and confusion of people praying with no meaning. The Lord manifested Himself through Olimpo's sincere, humble manner; and later that year 25 of his customers were baptized.

Christ has indeed promised us, "Lo, I am with you alway, even unto the end of the world." Often the faithful literature evangelist is surprised at the overwhelming success the Lord presses on him.

The Fabulous Talking Telephone Poles

On another occasion, the Holy Spirit impressed a little Japanese girl with a radically new way to tell the good news.

She was a lonely Seventh-day Adventist who knew what persecution is. How could *she* spread the gospel?

In her little room she wrote out Scripture texts on pieces of paper. At night she slipped out and tacked them to telephone poles around the village, something like handbills or notices of garage sales. Night after night she changed these written messages, presenting various truths of the Word.

Day by day the Buddhist villagers read the strange words, wondering where they came from. Finally a policeman stood watch and caught her. "Come tomorrow morning and meet me here," he ordered.

Next morning a crowd gathered and he introduced her, encouraging her to tell the people more. That little girl and her talking telephone poles raised up a little church on that Japanese island!

In America, Green River ordinances, which prohibit door-to-door selling, are sometimes invoked to stop literature evangelists. One brother was hauled before the local city fathers. When he explained how his books and magazines inspire young people to develop better values and avoid delinquency and drug abuse, one of the town fathers said, "This city needs more people like you. Our police will protect you. If we had more people like you, we wouldn't need so many policemen. You are worth as much to this city as six policemen."

When "No Sale!" Meant Time to Win Some Souls

I was making a call at a humble country house where no one seemed to be home. It must be that my angel impressed me to go around to the back yard. As I walked by a little shed, I noticed a window; and there inside a man with a beautiful white head of hair was bowed in prayer. I will never forget the sight. I knocked quietly on the door. I saw quickly that he was not going to buy, so I sent up a little prayer, "Lord, help me to do something for this man before I leave."

Then he began talking. "Young man, I would like to say something serious to you. I hope I won't offend you.

"When you go out doing work like this, you ought first to study your Bible and teach the people the truth. You see, young man, you teach people to keep the wrong day. The Lord's day is the Sabbath, not Sunday."

I asked, "Where did you learn this?"

"I have read my Bible," he said. "I also have a book, *The Great Controversy*."

"I too am a Sabbathkeeper," I assured him; "I too find that same truth in my Bible, and I too love that same book, *The Great Controversy*."

He seemed stunned. "Let me tell you some more, young man," he added. "When Jesus comes, He will find a small group of people, not vast numbers, who have His faith and keep His commandments."

I interrupted again. "I belong to a group like that. Next Sabbath I will be coming by here to meet with that group nearby. Will you come with me?"

Then I saw a light in his eyes. "Why, yes. This is too good to be true. I must be dreaming. Is there a group like this that I haven't known about?"

The next Sabbath I sat beside this dear man in that little group in Ironwood, Michigan. One Sabbath soon after, the pastor baptized him. When he came out of the water, dripping wet, he came straight for me and gripped my hand. "Now, I am happy," he said.

When we came back from overseas duty 15 years later, I found that he had gone to his rest. But I learned that he had let his light shine. He had gone up and down those valleys giving out literature and telling people of the message. Now there is a church in Ironwood.

You'd Never Guess Who the Lord May Send to Help You!

We received a letter from a Lutheran Sunday School teacher, telling how our books were helping her and the children. Then she urgently asked that we permit her to sell our books.

We responded as we often do to such requests, by sending a Voice of Prophecy card and suggesting that if she were to take this correspondence course and believe and accept what it teaches, that she could then apply for employment as a literature evangelist. She wrote back later, "I am studying and I am willing to live up to all I learn so long as it can be proved from the Bible. But now, don't put me off any longer. I want to share these books with my friends and neighbors."

Selling Books Without Having to Say a Word

Hulda of Tanzania thought the deluxe edition of *The Desire of Ages*, with its attractive picture of Christ on the cover, was such a special volume that it should not repose in her briefcase with more ordinary books. One day she was walking down the street, carrying her briefcase in one hand and *The Desire of Ages* in the other so that the picture of Christ could be seen. A non-Christian Asian lady stopped her and asked, "Are you selling that book?"

"Oh, yes," Hulda answered. The lady examined it briefly and bought it then and there for cash.

Stories come in from all around the world telling of a similar hunger for the truths in those wonderful books. Catholic nuns in Ireland and elsewhere read Uncle Arthur's stories to their students. In Mexico, two students contacted 25 Catholic priests one summer and sold 23 of them sets of our books. Catholic priests are hungry for God's Word also.

In addition to Catholics and Lutherans, some Pentecostals are ready to help us sell our books. Lance O'Neill of South New Zealand met such a family and sold them several sets. The husband gave him the name of another Pentecostal friend who he thought might be interested. Lance called on him and sold a set. Now he takes his Adventist books to Sunday School and puts on a display.

The Lord impresses many pastors of non-Adventist churches to cooperate with our gospel messengers. Raul Perez of Puerto Rico tells how he made a presentation of our books to a Protestant church group known as Defenders of Faith. The pastor himself introduced Raul as a Seventh-day Adventist, recommended *The Bible Story,* and later accompanied Raul to the homes of his people, encouraging them to buy.

Of course, not everybody says Yes to the literature evangelist's appeal. Many religious leaders try to discourage the faithful messenger. But it is important to remember that Christ's promise to be with us holds good *every time*, whether the people receive us or not. It's not *we* who sometimes get turned down at the door—it is Christ Himself, who is with us. Realizing this saves the literature evangelist from discouragement. He can then press on to the next door, confident that something precious will come out of every experience and that he will indeed find those receptive lost sheep that the Good Shepherd is longing to find.

Getting Through to People in High Places

The four-star general over all the armies of South Korea was gracious as we approached him with our books. After the sale was made and the money received, we ventured to ask a question: "General, we noticed that you purchased several copies of some of the books but only one copy of the book *Education.* Why is this?"

"You see," he replied, "these are being sent to my generals. But a top leader has to have some things that his men don't have, so this one book will remain in my office." We smiled at his sagacity and thanked him for the visit. When we left, we didn't know that we would be back in his office very shortly.

Our young Seventh-day Adventist men in the army were having trouble for refusing to carry guns. Some of us who had met the general personally were asked to intercede for these boys.

"I wish I could help you in a more direct way," he explained. "But you see, my hands are tied. The policy of our military is that a man is not a soldier unless he carries a weapon of war. Even though I'm a general, I can't change the rules of the army." Then he smiled reassuringly. "I'll tell you what I can do. I will suggest to my commanding officers that they not enforce that rule."

Proclaiming Peace in the Turbulent Middle East

One of the "highways" we wanted to travel in the Middle East was to meet the king of Saudi Arabia. His private secretary, however, refused to let us have the interview we requested. I asked, "Where did you learn to speak such beautiful English?"

His dark eyes sparkled. "I have a degree from the University of Nebraska."

"Let's shake hands," I said; "I have just come from there. My last five years were in Lincoln, Nebraska."

In a few minutes we saw police cars and motorcycles arriving, and we stood with excitement. The king was arriving! The secretary came straight to us and said, "Follow me."

On this visitors' day the king went into a large room where guests take their turns for a quick interview with him. To our amazement and delight, the secretary placed me in a chair by the side of the king, and Youssif, publishing director of the Middle East Union, on the other side. Soon we were handed a small cup of herb tea—a symbol saying, "You are welcome. Peace to you. You have had tea with the king."

I returned the king's smile and we drank together. I started out by saying, "Your honor, King Khalid, the Home Health Education Service has some of the most important books in the world. We wish to share them with the people of your country."

After a few pleasantries he said, "Your books are welcome." To our surprise he stood from his honored place and shook hands with me. The interview was over. Before we left the palace we were each presented with an autographed picture of the king.

We went to see the Minister of Information to present the books for his approval and told him how the king had welcomed us and our books. We knew the books must go through the scrutiny of the Ministry of Information, and we knew this could mean a long wait for a letter of approval.

When it came, the letter was only an invitation to come and negotiate. Next was all the red tape of authorization from the Ministry of Foreign Affairs and the Department of Trade. Finally we had to find a book store or agency that could bring our books in. Sad to say, we still don't have an agency willing to import our books legally.

But there is a back door open just a crack to let us get some books into Saudi Arabia. Many of the wealthy people of these closed countries visit Alexandria and Cairo for their vacations. Egyptian literature evangelists and students during school holidays sell our books to these vacationers, who take the books back into their homelands. One day the lamps will go on "like streams of light" all over those lands.

Many prominent Muslims in the Middle East are fascinated with the character of Jesus. One day in Cairo we found ourselves in a plush living room where a very kind lady readily purchased our books. Before we left, I was impressed to say, "Madam, I know you are a Muslim, but would I embarrass you if I invited you to purchase the best book ever written on the life of Jesus?"

"No, I will accept your challenge."

After we left, the literature evangelist with me said, "Do you know who that lady is? She is the most famous actress-singer in Egypt."

Another time we visited the top floor of a huge apartment building guarded by heavy security. This family had many books. We were sitting in the presence of the daughter of the late President Sadat of Egypt. She purchased a copy of every book we had in the briefcase. As we left she concluded, "Please come again and share your books with me."

Literature Evangelists Help Presidents

Norman Hepner, a courageous literature evangelist, has even given a book to the President of the United States. He stepped up to an aide, said, "I have a little gift for the President," and showed him a beautiful book. Approval was given, and as the President passed by, our book was placed in his hand. A word of gratitude was expressed, and another seed of truth was planted.

Getting to the President of Korea was an easier task. A retired Korean pastor looked like an ambassador as he and I sat like VIPs in the back seat of a car with an American driver. We drove right in past the guards at the gates, and they didn't even ask if we had an appointment with President Pak of Korea.

The secretary to the President welcomed us warmly. Our visit took only a few minutes, and the President became the happy owner of some of our precious books. We thanked the Lord that He had permitted us again to get behind security doors to meet someone in high position. Who but literature evangelists have such a privilege? "Do you see a man skilful in his work? he will stand before kings; he will not stand before obscure men" (Proverbs 22:29, RSV).

Sometimes They Have a Bit of Heaven on Earth

Anja Lakaniemi of Finland had a foretaste of the joy to be experienced by many literature evangelists when Jesus returns. In 1945 Oivas Heikkila, a judge of the Finnish high court, bought a copy of Maxwell's *Our Wonderful Bible* but didn't read it for many years. He had been active in the the church. Finally he took the book from the shelf. Then he met Anja and bought *The Bible Story*. Later he bought the complete Conflict of the Ages set and read all five volumes.

He read *The Great Controversy* three times. Then he attended an evangelistic campaign held in his neighborhood. Now deep conviction seized his soul as he wrestled with the call of God. When he yielded to the Holy Spirit, a sweet peace filled his heart. On the day of his baptism he gave five copies of *The Great Controversy* to his children.

One diligent young literature evangelist in Rwanda was beaming with delight at his wedding as he welcomed a number of very influential people and government officials as his guests. People were asking, "What has this young man done that all these prominent people attend his wedding?"

He explained to them, "I am indeed an important man, thanks be to God, because I am doing the most noble work in the world. 'If there is one work more important than another, it is that of getting our publications before the public, thus leading them to search the Scriptures ' (*Testimonies for the Church*, vol. 4, p. 390). You see, I have sold books to these people, and they have become my personal friends."

Faithful literature evangelists in East Africa have carried the good news into their "highways." Somebody among them made a deep impression on the mind of the President of Tanzania, Julius Nyerere. At a large gathering for the opening of a new government project, he said: "We have among us a group of people who are careful with their health. They do not use tobacco or alcoholic drinks. They keep our laws, are hard-working even though they rest on Saturday, their Sabbath. If all of Tanzania would follow their example, we could make this country self-sufficient."

Our books have also made a unique impression on President Daniel Arap Moi of Kenya. When Pastor Bekele Heye of the Eastern Africa Division took a delegation to meet him, he challenged the group: "Do you read the writings of that little lady, Ellen White, as I do? Her book *Education*, written long ago, is newer than today's school system. We would like to pattern our system after that counsel." Perhaps these books have helped this noted African leader to articulate the deep conviction, which he often expresses: "The government cannot *grant* religious freedom; it is already the fundamental right of the people."

Our Lord has commanded us to "go... into the highways" and give the gospel invitation to people in important positions. Some literature evangelists shrink from this challenging task. But those whose faith nerves them to do it often meet with thrilling experiences.

For now, all that any of us can have is a slight foretaste of the joy unlimited yet to be known when the Lord smiles at His faithful servants and says, "Enter thou into the joy of thy Lord." To have spent one's life in His service—how can one estimate such a priceless privilege?

"Our publishing houses are God's appointed centers, and through them is to be accomplished a work the magnitude of which is yet unrealized. There are lines of effort and influence as yet by them almost untouched in which God is calling for their cooperation" (*Testimonies for the Church*, Vol. 7, p. 144).

They Walk With Angels

A mysterious phone call at midnight awakened Lillian Ngaruiya, a literature evangelist in Nairobi, Kenya. A sweet, melodious voice said, "Please take a copy of *The Triumph of God's Love* to Mr. Kamau on the third floor of the Kencom building. Consider it urgent." The voice was gone and the phone went dead.

The next day Lillian went to that huge building only to be told that there was no Mr. Kamau on that floor. When she inquired up and down the building, secretaries all over were asking about the mysterious Mr. Kamau. Finally one sent for Lillian and confided to her, "My boss's name is Kamau, but he operates under another name." He was the deputy director of Government Corporations. Soon Lillian was ushered into his spacious office.

"Mr. Kamau . . ." But he stopped her short.

"My name is not Kamau!"

She continued, "Last night I received a phone call asking me to visit your office."

"No, you couldn't have received a phone call about me, for my name is not Kamau. Nobody knows me by that name."

Lillian opened her briefcase and took out *The Triumph of God's Love.* Looking him in the eye, she said kindly, "God knows your name—it is Kamau. It may have been an angel from heaven who called me, but he knows your name."

"There are no such things as angels."

Lillian said, "Mr. Kamau, let me tell you an experience one of my friends had, and you will know that there are angels. This friend does the same work I am doing, except she works in poor homes. One lady said, 'I like the book, but I have only half enough money.' At that moment a stranger knocked on the door and was invited in. He spoke up, 'Go ahead and write the receipt; I will pay the other half of the money.'

"As my friend started to go to another home, this stranger went along with her. She asked him, 'Who are you? What's your name?' He replied, 'That's not important, is it?'

"In the next house, the same thing happened. The lady wanted the book but didn't have enough money. Again the stranger volunteered, 'I will pay the balance.' And then at a third house, the same thing happened. As the two were leaving this house, my friend stopped and demanded, 'Tell me, who *are* you?'

"He asked for a piece of paper," my friend told me, "and wrote something on it.

"'My name—*Daniel na Siku Zetu* (*Daniel and Our Day*).

"'My address—*Sabato ya Kweli* (*The True Sabbath*).

"'My village—*Vita Kuu* (*The Great Controversy*).' (These are the Swahili names of three of the books she was selling).

"When she looked up, Mr. Kamau, he was gone. She believes and I believe that was an angel."

Mr. Kamau sat in rapt attention. She continued, "Let me tell you another experience. One of our representatives was demonstrating these good books to a friendly family who invited him to stay for dinner. They prepared *two* places for him. After they had washed their hands, they asked, 'Where is your friend?'

"'My friend? I'm all alone.'

"'No, we saw someone with you.'

"'You must have seen my angel,' he replied. 'He works with me.'

"Mr. Kamau, we believe that was an angel in the form of a man."

The director quietly asked, "What do I do now?"

"Buy this wonderful book and study it carefully. You are a special person in the eyes of God." Mr. Kamau did.

The Once Dark Continent Is Becoming Light

The Christlike happiness that radiates from the faces of African literature evangelists indicates that angels do indeed work with them. Salome and Naomi approached a humble home in Kenya and were surprised when the lady of the house, her face beaming, came out to welcome them as though they were old friends. The two literature evangelists introduced themselves, but the lady said, "Wait, I want to tell you about the vision I had yesterday. I saw two angels coming to my home in the form of ladies, carrying bags. I was told, 'When they come, listen to them and accept their message.' I told this to my friends who work with me on the farm. And you two are the very ones I saw."

But not always is such a warm welcome an evidence that angels from heaven have inspired it. In southern Sudan a literature evangelist was working in a village where prejudice was strong against our message. Our brother was surprised that in one home he was given an unusually warm welcome. He was even urged to have some food, for the people said he must be tired and hungry.

"Please be seated while we bring you some food," the strangely gracious hostess said. While he waited, he noticed some tension, although the host tried to keep the conversation going. He heard whispering from the kitchen. When the food was finally brought in on a tray, it was set on a low stool where the literature evangelist was sitting near the open door. The literature evangelist was impressed to ask the host to kneel with him for prayer. He prayed an unusually long prayer, asking God to bless the family and the people in the community, on and on, before he finally asked God to bless the food provided for him.

When they opened their eyes, a straggly little dog was eagerly gobbling up the food. The host chased the animal out and apologized profusely. The dog lay down outside, whimpered, turned around in a circle, and then began to whine pitifully. Our literature evangelist quickly excused himself and went out thanking the Lord for saving him from an excruciating death.

That poor dog died in place of a literature evangelist, but another dog was sent by an angel to help one of the Lord's servants in Tanzania. She possessed a precious new bicycle that she treasured. One night a burglar broke in and took everything she owned.

She quickly told the neighbors. Shortly after, someone came running. "We have found all your things left by the side of the road." Standing by was a strange dog. Evidently he had frightened the thief. He guarded the things until they were returned to the rightful owner. No one had ever seen the dog before, nor was it ever seen again.

The Repeated Mystery of an Extra Stranger

Puzzled customers frequently tell of seeing an extra person accompanying our literature evangelists. Tu Han Kim of Korea was canvassing in the rice paddies when he met a dignified grandfather, who purchased some literature. Brother Kim then prayed with the old man and went on his way.

Soon the old man came hurrying across the fields to the pastor of the local Seventh-day Adventist Church. "Something is wrong! Maybe there is a spy here. I saw *two* men coming to me, but then there was only one! And after I bought the literature, I saw *two* again!" Our pastor said: "I know the man who talked with you. You must have seen his guardian angel."

Pedro Rodriguez and Clemente Benitez of East Venezuela canvassed together on the Caribbean island of Margarita. They walked over the entire island, contacting every family and even sold literature to three Catholic priests.

One day they called on Petra Anes, principal of an elementary school. They asked for a drink of water. To their surprise, she brought four glasses instead of two. Later Petra explained it to an Adventist friend.

"I actually saw *four* men come to my house, and my servant girl also saw *four*. Two were dressed in white and two in ordinary clothes. When the servant girl brought the water, she was surprised, asking, 'Where are the other two men?'"

Paulien Wurarah and four other literature evangelists in East Indonesia were working in a Muslim area where prejudiced people turned them away. But the villagers began reporting that they saw *six* of these evangelists. Word began to spread through the community that an angel of God was working with these five. Soon the people began *asking* for our books.

A Zimbabwe literature evangelist tells of a harrowing experience he went through during the ordeal of violence in that once-troubled land. A gang of rebels ambushed him. "If you will promise to sell only your medical books and leave those cursed religious books," they warned him, "we'll let you go."

The literature evangelist replied, "I can't be dishonest and make a promise I can't keep. God called me to this work, and I must spread His special message."

They started a fire with pages torn from his books, and then threw all of his books, magazines, tracts, and even his briefcase into the fire. Then they beat him and left him for dead.

When he regained consciousness, all he saw of his books was the pile of ashes. How could he ever get started again? Stumbling through the bushes, he saw a man who called to him, "What happened to you?" Thinking it was another rebel, the literature evangelist was at first afraid. But the man seemed kind, so the literature evangelist told his story. The stranger gave him a Zimbabwe note valued at about a hundred dollars and said, "Go buy some more books." Then the man was gone. Our literature evangelist knelt down to thank God for this blessing.

As he came to another clearing, he saw another stranger who asked the same question. This man gave him another similar note and said, "Go buy more books," and he was gone.

God's angels surely know where Zimbabwe is, for they have often had to work there. Another literature evangelist was caught between the local fighting forces but tried to keep on selling his books. He called on a man who turned out to be a guerilla, cleaning his gun.

The man said, "Just a moment, and I will help you." He came back with a handgun, saying, "I am going to kill you."

Our literature evangelist was too shocked to say a word. He just sat still and prayed.

Shortly the man exclaimed, "All right, I'm not going to shoot you." There was another long silence. Then the man spoke again. "I see that big man who came to help you. We won't start a little war here. You may go now."

Angels help our African literature evangelists who are often so poor that they live virtually from hand to mouth. Many sell a few books before they can even eat, then they sell a few more. One was sick for a week, unable to work. He stepped outside his door. On the wings of the wind came a

20-shilling note. He believes an angel brought it to him just when he needed it most.

Heaven Has a Special Care for Literature Work

Guerillas and political rebels in many disturbed Third-World lands give angels plenty to do because our literature evangelists are undaunted in their efforts to spread the good news of Christ's love. A young man in the southern Philippines was returning home at dusk after a busy day delivering our books. A short distance outside his village he was attacked by rebels who knocked him to the ground and stabbed him repeatedly. One rebel, no doubt a Roman Catholic, lit a candle and stuck it in the sand alongside his body, signifying death. The four rebels then disappeared into the jungle.

A few minutes later a passerby saw the candle and hurried up to see what had happened. He recognized our literature evangelist and rushed to call his parents, who carried him to the nearest hospital.

While the doctor and nurses worked on him, he regained consciousness for a moment and said, "Don't be afraid, I'm not going to die. I am a worker for the Lord and my work is not finished yet." Then he lapsed into unconsciousness again. He remembers awaking a second time and hearing the doctor say, "Son, I am an Adventist doctor, and I will stay with you night and day until you are well again." While the doctor was speaking, the literature evangelist could hear voices singing, "Stand Up for Jesus."

After many weeks of convalescing at home, he returned to the hospital to thank the staff. He asked to meet the Adventist doctor, and he was told that no Adventist was at the hospital and never had been.

In an Eastern land, the government had closed our publishing house. Some of our believers operated little printing presses in secret places, producing Sabbath School quarterlies and other simple literature which had been banned.

Samuel Yung had such a press under his house. One day a search party came to investigate. A very large man came out of his house and started to run. The police chased him, yelling, "Stop, or we'll shoot." He kept running faster and faster. They kept after him, but he outran them and disappeared. This stranger distracted them long enough for Brother Yung to hide his equipment.

God's servants don't always realize the presence of holy angels with them. Nonetheless, God's promise is abundantly fulfilled for each one. "He shall give His angels charge over thee, to keep thee in all thy ways. They shall bear thee up in their hands, lest thou dash thy foot against a stone" (Psalm 91:11, 12).

When Holy Boldness Gives Success

With the exception of religious freedom for those Christians who already live there, most of the countries of the Middle East are closed to Christianity. The law forbids proselytizing, and a Muslim who changes his faith must be stoned. This makes it very difficult for a literature evangelist to get permission to enter such a country.

The secretary to the consul was giving our very capable literature evangelist, Youssif Farag, the typical run-around when he was applying for a visa to a certain country. So Brother Youssif smiled and said to him, "Friend, you should get up now and go into the rest room."

The secretary asked, "Why?"

"Because I am going in to see the consul, and you won't want to see me."

The secretary said, "Oh, no, no, no! I can't give you permission to do that. You must not."

Youssif smiled again and said, "Sir, if you don't want to leave, just duck your head below the desk or shut your eyes so that you won't see me. I don't want to get you in trouble, but I *am* going in and it would be better if you didn't see me."

The secretary tried to stop him. Whereupon Brother Youssif smiled again and said, "I'm warning you. Shut your eyes." He turned, made a light knock on the door, and walked in.

The consul was surprised, and more surprised when Brother Youssif spoke in Arabic, "Ahalin, wa sahalin," and sat down. Brother Youssif tried to make friends with him quickly and then said, "I am doing a special work with literature for your people and I need a visa." He quickly introduced his literature, but he realized he was getting a negative response. So he said, "Call the ambassador before you tell me Yes or No!"

No one turns Youssif down easily, so the consul called the ambassador. After the visa was granted, Brother Youssif apologized to the consul for going over his head. He had already been to the ambassador and sold him a medical book.

Twenty-Seven Times in Jail

Youssif's canvass for a small or large sale only takes about three or four minutes. Often he says something like this, "If we would charge you for the knowledge in this book, or if we had to pay the people who wrote it for us, it would be very, very expensive, in fact nearly impossible for you to purchase it. So you see we are almost giving it to you. Would you be able to use it best in English or in Arabic?"

Most people in Egypt read very little English, so Youssif and the customer smile together. Youssif gets his receipt pad out. In lightning speed he writes the name of the book or books and the amount, tears off the receipt and hands it to the individual, saying thank you with a big, magnetic smile of confidence.

It is not unusual in an apartment building for him to ring two doorbells at the same time. If both answer, he says to one, "Oh, I'm so sorry. You wait just five minutes and I'll be right back."

One lady stopped Youssif as he was leaving the apartment building and pleaded, "Please come back and pray with us again." Another family, when they saw him a few days later, entreated, "Please come and pray in our home again. Things have gone so well since your prayer." Another said, "Will you please write that prayer down for me? It was beautiful!"

Youssif has been behind bars 27 times. Through the sale of books to the wife of President Nasser of Egypt, however, he won her friendship. This no doubt saved him many times in that Muslim country.

Aráb Literature Evangelists Can Teach Us What Bold Faith Is

One Arab literature evangelist was working in the large apartment buildings of Cairo, Egypt. He became friends with the guard at the entrance, made his way to the top apartment, and worked down, selling to nearly every family. He had placed 12 large books with 12 families. Since he had not called on every apartment in the building, he went back the next morning to finish.

Sitting by the guard was an Arab sheik in his white robe and white headdress, looking like an angel. But he didn't look happy. He was holding 12 large books on his lap!

With almost a trembling voice he said, "We are giving you back these books. These are Christian books. We want our money back."

The literature evangelist tried to reason with him, telling how the books are for everyone. Finally, the Muslim exclaimed, "Well, either you take these books back, or I am going to take you to the police!"

When a Christian in a Muslim country has been proselytizing among Muslim people and is taken by a Muslim to the police station, he can be in deep, deep trouble. Almost anything can happen.

Our literature evangelist didn't give up easily. He continued to try to convince the sheik of the value of the books. When he saw he was fighting a losing battle, he said, "All right. I will give you *your* money back—for *one* book. You bought only *one* book."

"Then," said the bitter, irate sheik, "we'll go to the police."

More fear came when the literature evangelist learned that the chief of police was in. There was no time for delay. The moment of reckoning had come. The literature evangelist took the lead, went to the door of the chief, knocked lightly, stepped inside, and greeted the chief politely, thanking him for the courtesy of allowing them into his office. He introduced himself and his Muslim companion, said a few words to make the chief friendly, waited a few seconds until the chief asked them to be seated, then went straight into his canvass.

He showed the chief how there is a problem, and how he therefore has a need. He brought out his book, presented a few of its benefits, and called for the order by saying, "Do you prefer it in English or Arabic?" The chief readily purchased the book. The literature evangelist thanked him profusely. Then, turning to the sheik he asked, "Do you have anything to say before we leave?"

There was silence for what seemed like a long time, then the sheik slowly shook his head, saying, "No, I guess not." They both shook the chief's hand, bowed, and went out. The literature evangelist led the way out of the station, down the street, back toward his canvassing territory. There was no talking, just two dignified figures walking down the street, one dressed in white carrying a stack of 12 books and God's humble servant walking along just ahead of him carrying the briefcase. It was very evident to all passers-by that they were on a very important assignment.

Before they got back to the big apartment building, the sheik broke the silence. While holding those 12 books on one arm, he put his other arm around the literature evangelist and said to him affectionately, "You are a good man! Today you will come to my house and have dinner with me." And so he did.

"The righteous are bold as a lion" (Proverbs 28:1).

The Irresistible Influence of Literature

Late one Sunday evening I called at a Catholic home. The parents insisted that I sell them only *The Bible Story* set. I told them, "It's against my religion." We laughed.

They said, "Well, it is against our religion to buy the big books." We talked a long time. I told the children many stories. Finally they said, "Well, there is no need to talk. It is either *The Bible Story* alone or nothing." So I gave in and signed them up for the set only and for the Voice of Prophecy correspondence course.

At Christmastime I received a card saying, "Dear Uncle Thomas: May you have a happy Christmas. Thank you for the books. They are such a blessing to our home."

Some months later the Fargo church pastor wrote, "By God's grace, I baptized Mrs. James (Paulette) Wilm this past Sabbath, July 26. Her husband threatened to leave her. He didn't, but he's giving her some opposition. We're praying and working tactfully, seeking, by God's grace, to win him to Christ.

"You remember, you sold this lady some books and enrolled her in the Voice of Prophecy course. She took the course and was greatly blessed. I received her name when she finished and enrolled her in the Gift Bible course. She loves to study the Scriptures and deeply loves her Lord. I knew you'd rejoice to learn this bit of news!"

Later I spoke at the Fargo church and found her there, beaming with joy and with many stories of victory.

The Children Called a Committee

It was very evident to the children that the literature evangelist had done his best to convince their mother to buy. He was about to leave their home and they were still not the fortunate owners of *The Bible Story*. So *they* called a committee.

The older boy asked the literature evangelist to wait just a moment. The children went quickly into the bedroom, had their little committee, and came back and announced to their mother, "We have decided to buy the books."

"And how will you pay for them?" she asked. "Have you decided on that?"

"Yes, we have decided that we are going to go without dessert until the books are paid for. You can use that money to make the payments."

The mother was shocked. "And have you decided where you will get the down payment?"

"Yes, we are going to take the money out of our banks." There was silence and silent prayer going up from the literature evangelist.

The mother saw tears in the literature evangelist's eyes and finally got her voice to say, "All right, children. We'll buy them."

Six months later the literature evangelist's phone rang. "Hello, this is Mrs. Moreland. The books are paid for, and we are having a little party with a very special dessert. Please, could you come and celebrate with the children?" Of course he could. I am sure the angels were also rejoicing.

He Prayed on the Priest's Steps

A literature evangelist heard this story from one of his customers: "Three weeks ago you wouldn't have recognized me. I was a nervous wreck, constantly biting my fingernails, smoking far too much, and drinking myself into the grave. I seemed filled with hatred, for this was what I showed toward my wife and four children. I couldn't understand myself; this condition grew and grew until I had to see my doctor.

"While I was waiting, I picked up a colorful book called *The Bible Story* and started reading it. I'd never read anything so wonderful, and from that book I began to realize that God had a plan from the beginning to save man. I can't tell you the joy that brought to me, to know that God cares about *me*!

"I was so thrilled over that book that I borrowed it and read it from cover to cover. What a message! I was convinced of God's love for me and knew I had to change my life, yet I was afraid to go to God. I felt too sinful. I was frustrated, not knowing where to go for help.

"My biggest problem was that I didn't know how to talk to God. Raised a Catholic, I never really learned to pray directly to Him. I decided to visit my priest and ask for help. But to add to my frustrations, he was eating dinner and couldn't talk to me.

"As I stood there on my priest's front steps, I remembered reading in *The Bible Story* of men who talked directly to God. If they could, so could I. I knelt right there on the steps and asked God to change my life. I told Him how much I wanted to stop smoking and drinking, and how I wanted to feel love toward my family instead of hatred. I dedicated my life to God right there, three weeks ago, and today I'm a new man. Look at my fingernails; I don't bite them anymore and I don't smoke either. I want to give my whole life to God. I want Him to take me and use me."

How a Tough Husband Was Subdued

A little boldness on the part of literature evangelist John De Cenzo was the means the Holy Spirit used to soften a hard heart. John tells the story:

"The directions on the referral card said, 'Down a dirt lane, past a big house.' The man had an oil-delivery service. The lady invited me in. She really liked the books but said she would have to talk with her husband.

"After several unsuccessful attempts, I finally found the man home about suppertime one evening. The lady met me at the door and said she had changed her mind, but I knew she didn't really mean it. From the other room a gruff voice shouted, 'We're not interested; if you don't get out right now, I'll take my gun off the shelf and come out blasting.' I left immediately.

"Some time later I was looking for someone to deliver heating oil to me. I remembered this man and decided to confront him. Did he remember me? Ah yes, he did; and he apologized! Then he asked me to call again and let him see the books.

"The day we visited him he was in his little office. At the conclusion of the canvass, his daughter came in from school. He asked her whether she liked the books, and she replied, 'Oh, yes, I do.' Then he called his wife, and she said she had always wanted them. He purchased the entire Home Library and told us he was interested in studying the Bible, since his mother had been a preacher. We enrolled him in the Voice of Prophecy Bible course. Then he mentioned that his accountant had suggested he donate more money to the church for a tax write-off. My publishing leader suggested he make a donation for Ingathering, which he promised to do. He also offered to mail out folders advertising *The Bible Story* to his 900 customers!

"By God's grace the tough husband who ran me off with a gun became a friend, a customer, and an advertiser for our wonderful books."

How Books Change Lives

Rock musicians are not normally receptive to gospel truth. But here is how one of them in Australia describes what our books accomplished in his confused heart:

"Just 12 months ago I was a drug-using, pleasure-loving rock musician, caught up in the never-ending cycle of waking and sleeping with no joy but to play my guitar and get stoned. I thought I was doing all right until an Adventist friend spoke to me about Bible truths. I asked him to show me more. That night he arrived at our caravan with three Bibles, a *Great Controversy, Unfolding the Revelation,* and *Steps to Christ.* He then went on to show us the prophecies of Daniel and Revelation and their fulfillment in our time.

"My girlfriend and I were amazed. We began keeping the Sabbath even while still smoking. Then I finished reading *The Great Controversy.* Now I am smoked out! This book opened my eyes. We started attending church July 31, were married September 14, and baptized in November. We want to thank you for the joy your papers and books have brought to our lives. We have found so much love and peace in Jesus through the written word. I am now yearning to help sell your wonderful books through literature evangelism."

Gakwerere Kimenyi of Goma, Zaire, traveled a whole day to reach the small town of Bunyakili. There he sold two books to a Pentecostal minister, *The True Sabbath* and *Daniel and Our Day.*

That pastor read the books and lent them to his church members. Soon there was great excitement in that community. When our brother next visited them, he not only sold more books but also had to answer many questions from interested customers. Soon a lay preacher was sent to help with Bible studies. In a short time the pastor and 33 members of his church requested baptism. We now have a church with more than 100 members in an area where nothing had been attempted previously. It is all the result of what the Holy Spirit can do through the dedicated work of one faithful literature evangelist.

A Stretched Tie and a Right to the Jaw!

Chuck Smutzer was canvassing in the little town of Alda, Nebraska. A lady told him that her husband wasn't a Christian and would be very unhappy if she purchased any books. As she looked at Brother Smutzer, she said, "Our children need these books and I am going to buy them." Just before leaving the home, Chuck prayed, enrolled her in the Voice of Prophecy course, and gave her some literature.

She said, "You might want to go down the street to a friend of ours." Brother Smutzer made a note of the name and went on his way. He showed the books to the lady's friend, who also purchased.

In the meantime the non-Christian husband of the first lady came home. He was infuriated. He called the city police and reported that this "book salesman" was down the street at the address his wife had given. As Brother Smutzer came from the house of the referral rejoicing because of the sale, the police pulled in behind his car and notified him of a city ordinance that did not permit people to sell from house to house. At this time the non-Christian husband pulled up behind the police car, came up to Chuck and threatened his life. The policeman got between the two and told the enraged man to get back in his pickup and go home, but he would not do so.

The police talked with Chuck concerning the ordinance and told him he would have to get into his car. As they were getting into the car, the enraged husband attacked Brother Smutzer, pulling his tie and hitting him on the jaw. Despite finding blood on his face and on the man's fist, Chuck felt no pain.

He was released on $150 bond, and a date was set for a court hearing. John Mason, George Dronen, Brother Smutzer, and I contacted the city attorney. As we unfolded to him the nature of our work and how we present literature that would be a blessing to their homes, he was very impressed. As he realized we offer a free Bible course to people, give away free literature, and pray with them before leaving, he could see that we were earnest in wanting to help people. He asked us to cease our canvassing in Alda until he could counsel with some of the city fathers.

The case was soon dismissed, the $150 bond returned, and a license granted to visit the families in their homes. Because the irate man's wife was determined that her children needed the books, even the first sale was saved.

"You Knew, but You Didn't Tell Me!"

A young literature evangelist sold a small book, *The True Sabbath,* to Mr. Lupambo in Zambia. The customer read the book and became so convicted of its truth that he couldn't sleep at night. "Are you sick?" his wife asked.

"No. It's that book. I can see that Saturday is the true Sabbath."

"You didn't know that? I've known that for a long time. The Adventist people go to church on Saturday. I went to their school and was a Seventh-day Adventist at one time." Then she gave him a nice long talk about how it doesn't make any difference which day you keep as long as you keep one and honor God. "I suggest that you just forget about it."

He tried to do as his wife counseled him. But he read the book again, and his conscience went to work again. He asked his wife, "Do you know where the people are who keep the Sabbath?"

"Oh, yes, they are everywhere. Would you like to go to one of their meeting places on Saturday? I will show you."

So they went together to our church in Lusaka. To Mr. Lupambo's surprise he saw people there he knew, people he worked with. He went up to one man and said, "What are you doing here?"

"I come here every week. I'm a member of this church."

"You never told me anything about this!"

"Well, you never asked."

Soon Mr. Lupambo was taking Bible studies. At the time of his baptism he said, "Just think of it, people who work with me and for me said nothing. How are the people going to know if *I* say nothing?"

Soon Brother Lupambo left his high, lucrative position to become a literature evangelist witness for Jesus Christ.

Called From the Plow

During World War II Kenneth Holland quietly lived his faith before his fellows in the army. One of his friends, Lou Ramirez, watched and admired him, but couldn't help harassing Ken when he knelt to pray.

Years later Ken became editor of *These Times* and *Signs of the Times.* Lou became a highly successful businessman.

When they met later, Lou said, "Ken, you are now shaking hands with your brother. I have learned to know the Saviour before whom you used to kneel so fearlessly. I have become a Seventh-day Adventist!"

Lou gave Ken a big hug. Imagine their joy as they talked of how the Lord had led them both.

One Sabbath while attending the Shadyside Church in Pittsburgh, Pennsylvania, Lou heard me speak of how God calls His workmen: "There is a man sitting here today—I don't know his name or where he's from—who is wondering, How would I know if God were calling *me*?" Then I listed the ways a person might know.

After the worship service, Lou shook my hand. "I am that man! You don't know who I am; but I'll tell you. I am a businessman from California, and I am wondering that very thing, How would I know if God is calling me?"

Afterward I visited him in his hotel. It was quite evident from the beautiful suite, the fruit on the table, and his attitude, that he was not an ordinary fellow. We talked a long time. When Lou left Pittsburgh, he had a written resignation in his briefcase from the position of the vice-presidency of his company. He would become a literature evangelist!

He was successful. Of course, he already had considerable sales training and experience and spoke both Spanish and English fluently. Later Lou became the Inter-American Division publishing director, and in 1980 this former Catholic boy, Luis Ramirez, became the world publishing director of the Seventh-day Adventist Church.

It is not only from the Roman Catholic Church that the Lord calls men and women to work in His vineyard. There is another communion that does not often present a hopeful field for missionary work—the Amish society. Paul Cordray was raised in an Amish home by his grandparents. He found the Seventh-day Adventist message and accepted it during his time in the U.S. Air Force.

Some years later, when Paul became a literature evangelist in Missouri, he "hit the ground running," as we say. During those first days of canvassing Satan tried to drown him when Paul attempted to ford a swollen stream in his car. His books, prospectus, and samples were lost, but, thank God, his life was spared.

Years later Paul and his supportive wife, Judy, served the Zambezi Union in Africa, the Trans-Africa and the Eastern Africa Divisions, and the Canadian Union as publishing director.

When the Price Went Up Too High

Ken O'Guin was a Tennessee steeplejack. He owned a gun which he lent to a friend, who used it in a robbery. Soon the police found who owned the pistol, and Ken found himself booked as an accomplice to murder.

Behind the bars this non-Christian boy looked up to God and said, "If You are up there and if You love me, show me and I will respond to Your love." God did love him, and Ken did respond. He was released without charges.

One day he brought home some pork. His wife Fran said, "The Bible tells us that we shouldn't eat pork." Ken stood up, and said, "Well, why didn't you tell me that before?" He went to the refrigerator, took out the unclean meat, and threw it in the garbage can.

Some time later Ken was sitting in the congregation of the Pontiac, Michigan, Seventh-day Adventist Church when the challenge came to become a literature evangelist. He started part time but very quickly became full time, for he was a man of decision. His readiness to make decisions often impressed his wife.

Now, the bravest men get discouraged at times. One morning Ken called my home, saying, "Russ, I'm through. The price has gone up on the books and they are too high. I can't sell them at that price."

I knew that this price rise was justified and that the Lord would not forsake His servants because of it. I said, "Ken, please wait for me. I will be right over." A man of action as he was, he was dressed and ready to go to work when I arrived.

I asked if the briefcase was loaded and he answered, "It is always loaded."

"Ken," I said, "I'm going to do all the work. If we sell a certain amount today, you buy a watermelon for us as a special treat."

"That's a super deal!" he exclaimed.

It was the biggest day of sales that Ken had ever had. The next day we set our goal much higher, and I said, "When we reach that goal tonight, I will buy the watermelon." It was 11 p.m. and Fran was still up waiting when our lights turned into the driveway to their house. Two very happy fellows got out, one with an empty briefcase and the other with a huge watermelon.

Apologize to the Nail Before Hitting It

On quite a number of occasions we urged carpenter Clair Pettit of Lincoln, Nebraska, to become a literature evangelist. Even though he was timid, he was a man of decision. As he was filling out his application, in answer to the question, "Do you think you could make a livelihood at this work?" he thought a long time, and with a determined look, wrote a great big Yes. He turned the application over and resolutely signed it.

When I took it to the publishing committee, the chairman, Floyd Sanders, said with a question, "Clair Pettit a literature evangelist?" Then he chuckled, "That man is so timid; I wouldn't be surprised if he apologizes to a nail before he hits it on the head."

But because of his deep consecration combined with hard work, Clair was a success from the start. He placed our precious books in the home of the pastor of the Church of Christ. Pastor Fred Morgan and his wife read their way through the volumes. They also read a story or two each night to the children. Soon Fred wrote a letter saying, "Please let me be a representative of your beautiful books." We signed him up for the Voice of Prophecy Bible course and sent a brilliant scholar to have Bible studies with him. They studied together long and hard. It was a struggle, but Fred was baptized one Sabbath, resigned his pastorate on Sunday, and started as a full-time literature evangelist on Monday morning in his home town.

Fred sold the town renegade some books and noticed one day in the paper that he was in the hospital from a very severe beating in one of his drunken street brawls. Fred visited him, and in his hospital bed the renegade gave his heart to Jesus.

His grandmother was in the hospital at the time. Immediately he started witnessing to his own grandmother, and she surrendered her life to Jesus. What a beautiful chain reaction!

From Pancake-Flipper to Selling Books Like Hot Cakes

Dan Gilbert of Denver, Colorado, was short of help at lunchtime in his busy pancake house, so he himself was seating customers as they came in. As he showed a couple to their table, he clearly heard a voice saying, "Dan, God needs you too." He was startled and a little frightened.

Dan's wife had been studying the message and had started to keep the Sabbath. He had threatened to throw preachers out of his house. He was fighting his conscience.

After the voice spoke to him, he couldn't concentrate on anything, so he turned the restaurant over to his assistant manager, got into his car, and drove straight home. Who should be sitting in his living room studying the Bible with his wife but the pastor! The pastor stood and greeted him, asking, "Is there something I can do to help you?"

Dan responded by saying, "Yes, there is." The pastor, who was steeled for the worst, was really shocked when Dan continued: "You can baptize my wife, and while you are doing it you can baptize me also!" It was only days after that when Dan was telling people, "I used to be a pancake-flipper, but now I sell books like hot cakes."

Surely many literature evangelists could write a book! They are certainly helping to write a modern Book of Acts. Listen as they exclaim, "I used to be a farmer putting seeds in the ground. Now I am planting seeds in people's hearts." "I used to be a nurse helping to heal people's physical bodies. Now I am helping to heal their spiritual bodies." "I used to be a mechanic helping to repair automobiles. Now I am helping to repair people's lives." Lanny DeVer says, "I used to be a singer entertaining people. Now I sing in many homes, and the books I leave are going to cause people to rejoice and sing praises to their God forever."

My brother Dick says, "I used to be a building contractor, building houses that will be destroyed. Now I am preparing people to enjoy the mansions on high." A lawyer in South America says, "I used to be an advocate, trying to help my clients win their cases; now I am pointing people to the great Advocate and Priest of the Most Holy Place." Brother Un in Korea used to say, "I was a law enforcement officer; but now I am teaching people how to keep the law of God." A career literature evangelist would say, "I used to be a school teacher but my time was tied up with only a few little lambs. Now I am helping thousands of children."

In Korea a humble literature evangelist called on the home of Pastor Pak, a Presbyterian minister. The pastor purchased and read the book and accepted the Sabbath message almost immediately. He didn't argue with the message. It's true; "God said it; I believe it; that settles it."

He resigned his post as pastor and became a good literature evangelist. During his days as a literature evangelist he raised a very precious son. As the missionaries left Korea during World War II, his son, C. U. Pak, was appointed the treasurer of the Korean Union. Because he was the financial officer of a so-called American church, he was taken prisoner.

After the war was over, even though he was a faithful member, his name was taken off the church books because he had been in prison, thus disgracing the church. He tried to explain to the brethren that it was because of his work for the church that he had been imprisoned, but they would not listen. So Sabbath after Sabbath he sat on the back row of the Seoul Hospital Church, thinking that if the church had barred him from membership, it would bar him from the pearly gates also.

During those sad days, Brother Pak stated, "God has done so much for me that even though I will never get to heaven, I will pay my tithe, honor and serve Him, and come to His sanctuary on the Sabbath day until I die." Later the situation was corrected and he was taken back in to full, honored membership.

Among the many different plows from which the Lord calls His workers is a category we would hardly dream of: A poacher illegally trapping wild animals in the African game parks.

Zakaria Fondo of East Africa says: "I thank God that I met Him in my youth. He never forgot me, and He called me when I had wandered away from Him. I was in the forest trapping these wild animals, when at 1 p.m., September 5, 1976, I heard a voice saying, 'This job you are doing is not proper for a Christian. It is like stealing and is unholy.' After this I cried for two hours. I saw that I should stop trapping God's creatures.

"I was far away from home, but I immediately returned, having made a promise to God that I would do literature work. Therefore, my friends, I ask you who want to be workers for God to come and join the literature evangelist force, for it is the best of all jobs."

Have You Done Well?

In Lusaka, Zambia, there is a large church where nearly 4,000 can gather. Dale Thomas was appealing to our people to be among those to whom Christ can say, "Well done!" He challenged, "If the Lord should ask you, 'What have you done?' would you say, 'Lord, I was a faithful member and lived a good life.' When Jesus comes, what will you have *done* to warn the people of a coming judgment and tell them of a Mediator who gave Himself for them?"

After the service a dignified man came to him and requested an interview. J. B. Mwinga said, "Today you were talking about *me*. Ever since my youth I have done everything I have wanted to do. I wanted to live comfortably; I wanted money; I wanted a nice house; finally I wanted a second wife. Then my conscience bothered me, and I wanted to come back to church. I have done that too. Now I am an elder. But you know, I can't think of anything that I have really *done* for the Saviour. Up to now it has all been for *me*. But now I want to do something for *Him*. I want to become a literature evangelist, go out, meet people, and invite them to go with me to the kingdom.

There have been happy days for Brother Mwinga in sales and souls since then. He delivered the largest single order of books ever sold in Zambia.

"Do You Believe That Stuff?"

Glenn Howell tells of desiring to be a pastor but of being prevented by a speech impediment. He decided he would try his speech ability on one-person audiences and determined to canvass until his speech improved.

One day he awakened a man from his sleep. In spite of the disturbance, the man invited Glenn in and listened politely to his presentation. Interrupting Brother Howell's canvass, he asked, "Do you believe that stuff?"

Glenn confidently assured the man, "Yes! I wouldn't be selling these books if I didn't believe in them."

With a cynical spirit the prospect said, "I have been to the university and I found out a long time ago that there is nothing to the Bible except fiction. You are wasting your time here because we are not interested." He continued, "But if you would like to come back some evening and talk to my wife, you are welcome. In fact, come and eat with us. We could have a nice visit, but we wouldn't be interested in the books."

Glenn went back and enjoyed some good food and fellowship. As he had planned and hoped and prayed, the wife became interested in the books he left behind after each visit.

She and her husband soon attended church with Brother Howell, and as a result of the books and Bible studies, they were *both* baptized. To everyone's surprise they both re-signed their jobs and took up work as literature evangelists.

Glenn's speech gradually improved. He enrolled as a theology student, but not alone, for his new friends and canvassing companions went with him! Today all three are working for God.

From Krishna to Christ

William Deynes of California tells of his journey from Hinduism to Christianity: "I grew up in a Catholic home but left the church and lived as a hippie. Searching for something to fill the emptiness in my heart, I became a Hare Krishna worshiper; but every time I bowed to their ugly idol, I heard a voice in my mind saying, 'Thou shalt have no other gods before Me.' I continued my search, trying the Rosicrucians, the Buddhists, pagan sun worship, and finally a cult of the devil. All of these religions promised salvation by works. I began to be afraid. My life was miserable. I hated everybody.

"Sometimes I thought, 'If I should die today, would I be ready to meet God?' Then I decided to try Christianity, so I became a Catholic with my wife and daughter. The still small voice spoke again, 'Thou shalt not bow down and worship idols or images.'

"One day my wife and daughter went on vacation, and I stayed home alone. I felt very empty, and praying to the

Virgin Mary didn't help. I went to see my mother, and she said, 'Son, I have been praying for you for 11 years. Go to your room, bend your knees, and ask God to forgive you.' This I did, and immediately I felt peace and joy in my heart. The heavy burden left me, and the prayer of the prodigal son became my prayer to my Father. From that day on, I found real happiness, peace of mind, and the only way of salvation —Jesus!

"My life changed immediately. At first my wife would have nothing to do with the church, but after two years she was baptized, and later my daughter also joined us.

"I left my job to become a literature evangelist because I wanted to tell everyone about the beauty of Jesus. In a little more than four years I have seen nearly 60 souls come to Christ through my efforts."

From Hippie to Minister of the Gospel

A hippie pad is also a place where the Holy Spirit can find lost sheep. A group of hippies in 1971 were making fun of a *Bible Story* lead card that Max had found. Jokingly, he said to the others, "I'll fill it in so they will have a hard time finding us. We'll have some fun with those preachers!"

A few days later literature evangelist Eva Moreland was on her knees asking the Lord to help her decipher this strange name and address. Up and down the street, north and south, she went until she found a seedy apartment building that might possibly be the address. She already guessed that the one who signed might be a hippie.

Down the dark halls she searched. Horrible rock music, bad odors, and revolting sights met her. What could she do here? But she remembered that Christ died for these people too!

Finally she found apartment 8 and knocked.

Inside, Eva started to show the books, but the young man stopped her. "Wait up. Don't go so fast. I want to see every page." So she had to return to the story of Creation, and go through page by page. After she told about the Second Coming and the destruction of the wicked, she saw tears on those upturned faces.

"God sent you here," Max said. "I sent that card in but I was just clowning around. I thought no one would find me. But here you are."

They bought the books and read them.

Later when Eva called she met a different Max at the door—a cheerful, clean, enthusiastic, sharp young fellow.

"Please come in and sit down. I must tell you something great. Since you were here, I decided to go to my parents' home in Iowa and let them meet my wife, whom they had never seen. And were my folks ever glad to see us! I don't think I ever saw them so happy!"

His wife joined in, "I didn't know there were such wonderful folks in the world. You see, I have never been wanted by anyone—only by Max."

"Yes, and do you know what?" Max asked, "I told them about you and what I am going to do to help finish the work so Jesus can come back," he beamed. "My father has arranged for me to go to Moody Bible Institute and study for the ministry."

Two more young people were reborn and on their way to help in God's work. They may yet find all the truths of the everlasting gospel for these last days.

Jet Bomber Pilot Becomes Literature Evangelist

Elias Nyagi finished junior college and wanted to go to Sweden for further education. But the Tanzania military sent him to Russia for flight training. He was there for four years and became a jet pilot.

Back in Tanzania he did a test parachute jump, but his chute failed to open. He realized that in a few seconds he would meet his end.

Just before his body plunged to the ground his parachute opened, but not enough to keep him from very severe injuries including many broken bones and a hand which never will be completely restored. His face was mashed into the earth and badly lacerated. He was flown back to Russia for medical care and facial surgery.

Now great fear came into him, which Elias feels came from the Lord. His commanders tried to encourage him to become an engineer, but he said, "No, I want only one thing. I want to go home." He returned to Tanzania, became a Seventh-day Adventist, attended a literature evangelist institute, and in 1984 became a full-time literature evangelist. Brother Nyagi states, "I realize the importance of this work. Many of my friends keep telling me, 'You are an educated man. You could do many great things.' They don't realize the importance of my work, but God knows and I know, and I am very thankful to be privileged to do it."

What One Book or Magazine Can Do

"My English father, a young civil engineer, worked for the British government in Calcutta, India," says Mervyn G. Hardinge. "One afternoon while my father sat on the train, he decided to quit smoking. He opened his compartment window and tossed out his cigarettes, lighter, pipe, and tobacco pouch.

"A year or two later my parents also decided to quit drinking alcoholic beverages. Soon after that a meat scandal was disclosed in the newspapers. 'Why don't we become vegetarians?' they asked each other. Mother sought everywhere for a vegetarian cookbook, but to no avail. My father marveled that he survived the next two years.

"One day an American lady was at the door selling religious books. Mother turned her down flat. But as the lady was closing the gate, Mother felt compelled to call out, 'If you have a vegetarian cookbook, I'll buy one.'

"Two weeks later the literature evangelist returned with the book. Mother was ecstatic! After paying for it, she stood at the door leafing through the pages of recipes. The lady asked, 'Do you know how to cook vegetarian food?'

"'No,' was Mother's response, 'do you?'

"'Yes,' replied the literature evangelist. 'Would you like me to help you?'

"The American lady came regularly to help Mother learn to prepare vegetarian dishes. A friendship developed. Gradually the visitor began to talk about the Bible as they stood by the stove. Mother grew interested, and then Dad also. In time both were convinced and were baptized.

"That's how the Hardinges became Seventh-day Adventists! Three of their children have spent their entire lives working for the church. But what if that literature evangelist had *only* sold the book and made no effort to form a friendship? What if she had no interest in healthful cookery? What if she had been too busy to cook and to teach my Mother?"

Many years ago some unknown friend sent in a subscription to our missionary magazine for Nathan and Mary Lane. Nathan was a Methodist lay preacher who thought he knew his Bible. He was especially prejudiced against Seventh-day Adventists.

Mary used the magazines with some kerosene to start the fire in her kitchen stove. But one morning she said to herself, "Someone is sacrificing to send us this little paper. If he ever asks me if we received the papers, I would hate to hurt his feelings. I'll just read one page before I start the fire today."

The article she read was about the Sabbath. She became so interested that she finished it. And there in front of her kitchen stove, she made her decision to keep the Sabbath.

But how could she ever tell Nathan? For three weeks she did her cleaning and baking on Friday and secretly kept the Sabbath.

One morning outside the house, Nathan saw a scrap of a magazine and picked it up. On it were some Bible references that interested him. He went to his study, got out his Bible, and looked up the texts. The result: He got down on his knees and made his decision to keep the Sabbath. But how could he tell Mary? She would think he was crazy. And what could he say to his congregation?

Going into the kitchen, he took Mary in his arms and told her he had something very serious to tell her. He begged her not to laugh at him. She might think he had lost his mind, but that was not so. She was alarmed and wondered what it might be—some terrible illness? Is our marriage in danger?

When he told her, she laughed out loud. That hurt him terribly. He was afraid she was ridiculing his new faith.

"No, Nathan dear. I'm not laughing at you. I'm full of joy. Haven't you noticed anything different around here the past three weeks? I was afraid to tell *you*! I read about the Sabbath in those magazines someone has been sending us, and I decided to keep the Sabbath."

Nathan Lane became a Seventh-day Adventist minister and brought hundreds of people into the message. His great-grandsons are fifth generation gospel workers—all because some unknown person sent them a subscription to one of our magazines!

Charles Reep tells of a book that bore fruit after 25 years:

"Doris Gayle had her Bible lessons filled in faithfully every week when I stopped by her home. When she finished the lesson on the Sabbath, I asked if it was clear to her. She replied, 'I believe the seventh day is the Sabbath because my Bible says so.' She picked up an old copy of *Bible Readings* and said, 'This book tells me about it.' She had been reading about the mark of the apostasy in one of the chapters.

"'Where did you get that book, Mrs. Gayle?' I asked. She didn't know the name of the person who had sold it to her 25 years before, but she said she was living in Portsmouth, Virginia, in a section called Williams Court. My heart jumped. I said, 'Mrs. Gayle, I canvassed every house in that area at that time, and I was selling that book. Maybe I was the one who sold that book to you!'

"I invited her to come to church with me. Today Doris Gayle is rejoicing in this blessed truth. Many times she has remarked, 'Brother Reep, I thank the Lord every day for sending you to my home!"

From Her Last Penny to a New Plenty

Frank Henderson of New Zealand called on an elderly widow who, because of ill health, was unable to earn her own living. He demonstrated *My Bible Friends* as a possible gift for her grandchildren. Then she told him her story.

Her only son had gotten in with bad company and had left home, taking all her money. He married and had two children whom she had never seen. She was now sick and very poor. Then Frank showed her *Your Bible and You,* and she gave him a five-dollar deposit, the book to be delivered in six weeks. This was all the money she had!

Two weeks later she phoned and urged him to bring the book immediately, as she now had the money. She had nearly starved herself in order to get it sooner. Her cupboards were bare, but she said, "Mr. Henderson, I need that book. I could not wait six weeks." Soon after, the Lord blessed her with a windfall of money and improved health!

A medical doctor once recognized that *The Bible Story* was not only worth more than money, but that it was worth more than any medicine he could prescribe. Mrs. Holden, a worried mother, decided to take her eight-year-old son David to the doctor. After a thorough examination, the doctor explained that the boy was suffering from a nervous breakdown. The cause was the recent tragic terminal illness of his father. He and his father had been very close.

The doctor told Mrs. Holden that David was too young for the usual drugs to assist in his recovery. Instead he prescribed a more effective treatment. "Go and get *The Bible Story* display volume from my waiting room." When she brought it into his office, the doctor continued, "Now fill out this information card and send it in. I want you to get these Bible volumes and read a story to David every night."

Mrs. Holden thanked the doctor for his advice. The next morning she phoned the nearest HHES representative and requested a demonstration as soon as possible. How thrilled this mother was to purchase *The Bible Story* with *Your Bible and You.* Each night she read a story to David. In six months he had fully recovered and was able to attend school again.

"Spiritualist" Books Win One Hundred

Sister Manuela, an elderly lady of the Brazil Union, tells this story:

Once, before becoming an Adventist, she was very sick. Her husband took her to a healer, who, after examining her, concluded that she was physically ill and mentally discouraged. She needed medication, he said, but before the medicine could help she must get rid of her mental discouragement. He gave her two books to read. "These books will help you," he said, as he handed her *The Life of Jesus* and *The Light of Prophecy in Our Times.* He had bought them, thinking they were Spiritualist books.

Mrs. Manuela, eager to get well, read the books. She was so inspired by their message that she was completely healed of both her physical and spiritual ailments. After reading both books, she, her husband, and 11 children became Adventists.

Through these "Spiritualist" books and the witness of the Manuela family, 100 people have been won to the Adventist message.

Books Produce a Murderer and a Minister

Brothers George and Jim Sherbondy were sent to foster homes. Jim got hooked on paperback novels and took as his hero Jesse James, deciding he would be like him. At 17 he was behind bars for murder, having killed a friend of the family, the sheriff who came to take him into custody for a minor offense.

George was sent to another home and learned how to love and give. The book *Patriarchs and Prophets* changed his life. He found the Saviour in the book and became a Seventh-day Adventist minister.

Years later both James and George found themselves serving in Colorado, the former in solitary confinement for having broken parole, the latter as a minister of the gospel. George pleaded with the governor of Colorado to be allowed to change places with James, that James be released and George serve out James' term. But his request was denied. Later James, again breaking parole, was shot dead.

George has lived a useful life for the saving of others. He now goes house to house with our literature.

Still Bearing Fruit After 45 Years

More than 45 years ago someone sold *The Great Controversy* throughout western Nebraska. At times he may have wondered how much good the books would accomplish. But he kept on, accepting by faith the assurance that "the results of the circulation of this book are not to be judged by what now appears" (*Colporteur Ministry,* p. 128).

In Denver, Colorado, John Fowler discovered a battered old copy of *The Great Controversy* sold by that Nebraska literature evangelist. A woman attending his meetings told the interesting details:

Her aunt purchased the book more than 40 years before, accepted its message, and was baptized. In spite of her husband's opposition, she remained faithful, and six of her children joined the church. Undoubtedly many of her descendants are now faithful and have helped others to accept the message. Only heaven will reveal all the results from the sale of this one copy of *The Great Controversy*.

One of those stormy nights with blowing, wet snow and slippery roads, Lyle DeReamer was making a call at the David Schuman home in Albert Lea, Minnesota. This Catholic family with three children purchased *The Bible Story* and enrolled in the Faith Bible course.

When Mrs. Schuman read the story in volume 2 about how God provided twice as much manna on the sixth day and none on the seventh day, the truth of the Sabbath dawned on her. Comparing the story with the Bible lessons and the Bible brought conviction to their hearts. They asked for more studies and were baptized. Many more families like the Schumans are waiting for someone to knock at their door with this thrilling message!

Literature Ministry Serendipities

Serendipity is defined as "the gift of finding valuable things not sought for." Sir Horace Walpole coined the word from a Persian legend about three princes from the town of Serendip who, with luck or sagacity, returned from each errand with an unexpected blessing.

When Columbus tried to find a way to the East, he stubbed his toe on America; when Edison tried to invent the electric light bulb, he discovered the phonograph; Alexander Fleming discovered penicillin by the mold that blew in the window, fell onto his culture plate, and killed the germs. Jesus said, "Seek ye first the kingdom of God, ... and all these things shall be added unto you" (Matthew 6:33). Christ stated the greatest serendipity!

Literature evangelist Wendell Springer went to collect some money from one of his customers who was not sending in her payments, but ended up arranging for Bible studies and later baptized the family. This was serendipity!

Student literature evangelist Darlene Simmons determined she was going to give the people opportunity to buy our literature. Not finding them home, she went back seven times, finally sold them literature, and later saw them baptized; that also was serendipity.

When literature evangelist Paul Grave had car trouble and took it into a garage for repairs, he sold the mechanic the only set of books he sold all day—a serendipity.

The Korean girl who gave a grandmother her seat on the bus and ended up selling a whole case full of books, and receiving an invitation to canvass the entire town with the blessing of the police, tasted a delightful serendipity.

"Don't Come When My Husband Is Home"

L. Russell Thomas was working with one of the literature evangelists in the Arkansas-Louisiana Conference. They contacted a very worldly, backslidden Adventist lady who was interested in the books and asked them to come back. "Now be very careful," she said, "to come when I tell you, for my husband will be away. If he is here when you come, he will be very rude and may even do you bodily injury. He hates preachers."

The fellows arrived at the specified time. She was not there to greet them, but the dangerous husband was. He invited them in and was cool at first but soon became very friendly. The Spirit of God impressed him to purchase literature and to sign up for the Voice of Prophecy Bible course. They even made plans to give him personal Bible studies. Very shortly thereafter the entire family was coming to Sabbath school, and the "dangerous" husband was accepting the message even more readily than his companion. The angels surely mixed up that family schedule so that the literature evangelists found a serendipity.

Even a Scrap of Paper

"What's this?" Daniel Zoo Zoo asked his classmate when he spied a pile of old Sabbath School Quarterlies in a dorm room they were cleaning. "I'll put them in my suitcase," Daniel decided, "and on my way home for vacation on the train I can have fun with them."

A few days later, bound for Yaounde, Cameroun, he took out the quarterlies and threw one out the window. People scrambled to get it and even fought over it. How he laughed! So he threw another one out the window, and another. What fun he was having! Then he began to realize that his quarterlies would soon be gone at that rate. So he started tearing off just a few pages and throwing them out the train window.

Four years later Daniel was canvassing as a student about halfway between his home and school. He met a mechanic with a picture roll hanging on the living room wall. Daniel asked, "Where did you get that picture roll?"

Happily the man answered, "I'm a Seventh-day Adventist. About four years ago as I was working on the railway a boy threw some papers out the window of a passing train. One landed at my feet. Curious, I picked it up. God spoke to me through that paper. I gave myself to Christ then and there and looked up the Adventist Church."

With tears in his eyes Daniel exclaimed, "I was that boy!"

Dark-Room Technique

During the Civil War in the Cameroun a Muslim was afraid he would be killed. A Christian man said to him, "Come to my house. I will protect you." The family hid him in a closet in their house. Time dragged on his hands so he asked if he could have something to read. They gave him Christian books, and he became interested in knowing more about Jesus. After the conflict was over, he went to a Jehovah's Witness bookshop, where he found a book that did not belong there. It was Robert J. Wieland's *For a Better Future*. What a serendipity! He found Christ and His

Sabbath and went to the Christian who had hidden him and asked, "Do you know that Saturday is the Sabbath?"

"Yes, I'm a Sabbathkeeper."

So he not only accepted Jesus as his Saviour but the Sabbath as well. He continued to study until he had found the full message.

"Oops! Wrong Door"

One morning when Gary Tracy was canvassing in Omaha, Nebraska, he met one of the coldest icebergs he had met in many a day. The prospect showed no interest at all. Before Gary even attempted a close, he realized that he had forgotten to put his receipt pad in his case. He asked the prospect to excuse him a moment, and expecting to go outside to his car, instead went through the wrong door into the family bathroom. A very embarrassed literature evangelist backed out quickly saying, "Oops, wrong door." This hit the prospect's funny bone, and he started to laugh. Gary laughed too. When he came back from the car, the customer was still laughing. He sweetened up and became a totally different person. To Gary's surprise he purchased a set of books. Gary had just gone through the door of serendipity.

Serendipity Extraordinare

Terry Kemmerer and Victor Oberholt were buddies at Union College, Terry, a backslidden Adventist, and Victor, a Catholic. Terry had gotten hooked on paperback novels and had lost his interest in spiritual life. His parents had prayed long and hard for him. They had done everything they could to encourage him to be baptized but without success.

Victor had studied the message with many different people. He had even studied with George Vandeman but had never taken his stand for Christ to join the church.

Then the publishing people came to the college, recruiting students and telling experiences of how these books help young people by teaching values, and help them avoid such pitfalls as drugs. Both Terry and Victor determined that they would like to help young people. Thus they went out canvassing during the summer.

When they were at the youth camp for the literature evangelist Summer Rally, the publishing leader, George Dronen, discovered that they were not baptized members of the church. George very carefully and kindly but firmly impressed on their minds that they had to be members of the church in order to do this sacred work. So both of them agreed, "That's no problem. If we have to be baptized to do this work, please arrange for our baptism." These two who started out merely to help others ended up helping each other and themselves—a double serendipity.

Three Months' Expenses Paid for by One Kindness

A student literature evangelist on a very crowded bus gave his seat to a tired lady. Three days later he unexpectedly called at her house. They were both very surprised to meet again. She bought a copy of every book he was carrying. Then she went into another room and brought out a little box, stating, "I have saved this money for something special. Now I have found the something special to use it for." She was delighted to give it to the student. It paid his expenses for the entire three months' school vacation and canvassing time. He went back to school with a good scholarship as the reward for one little kindness.

It Pays to Work on Stormy Days

Bernice Goetz was going to be a success as a literature evangelist from the start, because she liked people and believed they were going to buy. Therefore, she was not afraid to *ask* them to buy. One unbearably hot day I was working with her and asked, "Aren't you tired and hot?"

"No, these people are going to suffer in a much greater heat than this if I don't suffer this heat to save them," she replied.

Bernice was working house to house in a very humble area of Detroit. It seems that the more humble homes always have more money for religious books. She finally made it to one big house and was received kindly but was given the typical putoff, "Come back on such and such a day and we will talk with you."

When that day came, Bernice was miserably sick. And it was a stormy evening. She says, "I felt terrible. My head was splitting, but I had an appointment for God. So I stumbled out of the house and drove bleary-eyed. The family was quite surprised to see that I would keep my appointment on such a stormy evening. They received me kindly and readily purchased the books. When I asked them if they would like to have Bible studies, they agreed; and I arranged to give them studies every Tuesday night."

The whole family accepted the message and were baptized. Then the mother of the family decided she would like to be a part-time literature evangelist. So those humble homes were visited by the kind lady who lived in the brick house on the hill, knocking on their doors and telling them how she loves Jesus. What will be the results someday of the life of a person like Bernice Goetz?

Father Chases Daughter and Gets Caught by Serendipity

Evangelistic meetings were being conducted in Kenya, and the conscientious Kikuyu father of seven children warned his family, "We do not want you to go to those Jewish meetings." But 12-year-old Yumbora heard the music, was curious, and went anyway. There was quite a commotion around their house the next day, and Father became the self-appointed policeman to see that she didn't go again that evening.

Yumbora watched for her chance, and when it looked as if no one was watching she ran toward the meeting. But Father *was* watching, and he ran after her and caught her. Yumbora made such a fuss that soon a whole crowd of people gathered around them. While they were all talking at once, Yumbora got away from her father and ran into the meeting. Father went straight to the meeting, right in after her. But the meeting was already in progress, so he sat down in the back. I will take her out as soon as I can, he thought.

The leader stood up and asked, "Who brought a guest tonight?" The children chanted, "Yumbora, Yumbora, Yumbora!"

The leader asked, "Will Yumbora's guest please stand."

Now Father was really in a fix! A little ashamed of himself and yet proud that the children not only knew his daughter's name but that she was being honored tonight, he stood up. Now he had to stay through the meeting.

Yes, he got caught. The Holy Spirit did it. The next night he didn't worry about Yumbora, for he was watching for his own chance to sneak off to the meeting without his wife seeing. He was thrilled again with the message. Soon Mother and all the children were in the meetings. Father, Mother, and Yumbora were baptized. Father became a literature evangelist. Later he went away to Bugema College in Uganda. Today he is our Pastor James Mwangi in Nairobi, Kenya.

In Korea Brother Kim, a handsome young man with a crippled foot, had plenty of excuses not to do the work of literature evangelism, but he was determined to help spread the message.

One day he visited the principal of a large, private high school who was interested not only in the books but in Brother Kim also. "Where do you come from? Are you a Christian? What does your church believe?" They started a Bible study, which resulted in Brother Kim's going to the principal's home and teaching him the entire message.

Almost immediately the principal started keeping the Sabbath and telling the students about it in general assembly. He changed the school schedule to Sunday through Friday. On Sabbath they had Sabbath school and church, releasing the students to go home at 12:30. Brother Kim served as their Sabbath school superintendent and pastor until he had taught them how to conduct the services themselves.

More Unexpected Serendipities

One literature evangelist in East Africa wanted to start a branch Sabbath school. At night he was holding evangelistic meetings near a local bar. When the owner of the bar came to work, his bar was empty. "Where are the people?" he questioned.

"They are all over at the meetings," was the answer he received.

"I'll go over and get them," replied the owner. He was so fascinated with the message, however, that he accepted very readily, took personal Bible studies, and became a member of the Adventist church. And, of course, he closed the bar!

The Pastor Stole the Cards

A pastor of the Africa Inland Church saw a stack of Voice of Prophecy enrollment cards. "Those cards will not do any of their evil work, confusing people who already have their religion, if I dispose of them." So he took the whole stack, planning to burn them.

Curiosity got the best of him, however, and he decided that he would enroll in the course. As a result he accepted the Sabbath message almost immediately. It took him a little longer to accept the truth about the state of the dead and the punishment of the wicked, but he finally took his stand with God's people. After a long series of Bible studies, he was baptized and became a literature evangelist. Now he goes out signing up people for the Voice of Prophecy Bible course.

One of the most fascinating examples of serendipity in God's literature work is the story of the Sharp family. Literature evangelist Campbell was on his way to Alaska when he met Mr. Sharp in Yellowstone National Park. Sharp was a Nebraska farmer on his way to California for a vacation.

Both vacationers changed their plans and stayed an extra week to study the Bible together. Sharp saw that the Bible indeed teaches the seventh-day Sabbath and other precious truths that were new to him. His vacation trip to California became a Damascus Road for him. He returned to eastern Nebraska and raised up a church. His three sons, Norman, George, and John, planning at first to head for a Methodist seminary, instead became Seventh-day Adventist pastors.

How a Noble Purpose Can Be Achieved

Dr. Israel Recio of Antillian College has worked with many youth. He seeks to impart that priceless ingredient of education that mere book knowledge can never impart.

"I became convinced through personal experience," he says, "what selling our books can do for a person with a noble purpose in life. I served three years as a full-time literature evangelist and eight summers as an assistant leader for students. The Lord gave me the privilege of seeing 12 souls baptized through my literature contacts. A church was organized, and a school was put into operation. This brought fresh dimensions into my life.

"Now, as an educator, I receive two kinds of young people in my office, those who have specific aims and those who have no purpose in life. I advise them to see for themselves what they can do for this sick world by putting in the hands of the needy books that will open hearts to the light from heaven.

"One-sixth of our student body earn money for their studies by selling our books. We call it our main industry, because it produces our top workers.

"After observing the results in hundreds of young lives, I know there is no good purpose in life that cannot be achieved through canvassing. Some months ago I advised a young man without interest in anything to find himself by going door to door and sharing his life with others. Now he is a new man with a goal, talking about being a missionary. Canvassing put a purpose in his life."

What makes literature evangelism so exciting is the constant unfolding of a series of delightful serendipities. "All things work together for good" is the Bible name for a serendipity. The same heavenly Father who notices when a sparrow falls is concerned about the little things in the literature evangelist's daily ministry. The Lord is always sending little extra tokens of His grace, unexpected providences that some would call mere luck but which the child of God recognizes as heaven-directed.

When God's Leading Came Just in Time

My wife Faith and I arranged to spend some time in Colorado Springs canvassing with our son Kendall and his partner, Craig White. Unknown to us, we were there just days before an evangelistic campaign was to start.

We chose to canvass near the church. While Kendall and his mother were canvassing, they came to the home of a lady who appeared to be rough and tough. She was cordial and friendly but bought only two little books, *The Marked Bible* and *Steps to Christ,* both selling for only a dollar. Because of the visit, the prayer, those small books, and the invitation, she came to the meetings; and she was the very first one to take her stand!

The Dream and the White Pig

Bringing the Henderson brothers into the message was akin to the struggle one has with a big fish. They fought and flipped and nearly broke the line all the way in. But big fish are worth it once you win the battle! After a long, hard fight and much study, Jack and JG were baptized.

Jack was managing a big department store. When he was challenged to keep the Sabbath, he resigned and went into direct sales, where he was soon in a management position.

When Jack became a literature evangelist in the Chesapeake Conference, he went three straight weeks without selling. He even lost his first sale. How could he do that? A man shocked him when he told him that he was interested in buying the books, but Jack kept talking and the man changed his mind. "I'll never forget that one," Jack said. "I learned there is a time to stop talking and start writing." He learned well, for he became a very successful literature evangelist.

One time literature evangelist JG had a dream in which he saw cows backing out of a trench pool. (Usually you prod the cow through the dip as she is being treated for disease or ticks.) At this same farm he saw a little white pig eating at the pig trough. He told his wife and she said, "Oh, JG, it's just a crazy dream."

"No, it is not just a dream," JG said. "God is trying to tell me something." As he canvassed, he kept watching for that farm. And one day he found it! But the devil was there to try to scare him off. The husband was away. JG met some women, and one of them seemed as though she were devil-possessed. "Get out of here," she screamed at him, "or I'll shoot you." JG tried to calm her. Finally he tried to convince her by telling her, "I have a special message for you. In fact, God has shown me this farm in a dream." He told her about the little white pig.

But she interrupted him, screaming, "Get out of here, I tell you, or I'll shoot you."

"I would like a drink," JG interjected.

"Go to the well and get a drink, and then get out of here, I tell you, or I will have to shoot."

"What time will your husband be home?" he asked.

"He's home at night, but don't come back here or I'll shoot you."

Another day JG went back after first offering a special prayer, "Lord, please have that little white pig come out to the trough so I will know that I am at the right place and that You sent me here. Please protect me."

He went down the hill and across the stream. The lady yelled to her husband, "Here's that man that saw our farm in a dream. He must be Moses or a prophet or something."

The Spirit of God took over, and they listened attentively and decided to buy *The Desire of Ages,* and *The Great Controversy.* Then as suddenly as they had decided to buy they changed their minds.

JG prayed again, "Dear Lord, let that little white pig come out to the trough again." Just then a little white pig appeared by the trough. The Spirit of God took over, and the people believed. One went out and dug up their hidden money chest, enabling them to pay cash for the books.

Dave Sandavol was shown in a dream the face of a truck driver who, he was impressed, was a searcher for truth. From the dream Dave knew the area, so the next day he started looking for that place. No doubt his angel guided him, for when he arrived at the spot there was the scene he saw in his dream—the truck and the driver.

He may have startled the man a bit, because he was so excited. "Stop," he called, "I saw you in a dream." Then he proceeded to explain to him what his work was about. Right there on the road he sold him a set of books.

Another faithful literature evangelist called on a house in split-second providential timing. A discouraged man was delayed in his suicide attempt. The angels got us to the right place at the right time. Just as the literature evangelist knocked on the gate, the man cut his wrists. It was a messy visit, but a life was saved in the nick of time.

Once it was an earthquake that came just in time. A literature evangelist couldn't get the attention of the prospects, but just as he said, "In the last days there will be earthquakes. . .," a violent earthquake shook the house. He had their attention, and they bought the book. Together they prayed and thanked the Lord for His protection.

On another occasion the Holy Spirit delayed preparation for death. "The minutes ticked by," Jeanette Scholes explains, "as I presented *Your Bible and You* to a prospect. She seemed unconvinced of her need and said, 'I have no money to purchase the volume.' I was leaving the house when she called me back. After a few words of discussion she said, 'I'll take that book.' As I was writing up the order, she added, 'I'll pay it all now'; and bringing out a purse from another room she said, 'I've been saving up for my funeral. I'll just take the money from that.' I think she got the money from the appropriate fund," Jeanette says. "The undertaker can wait for this woman to find eternal life."

When Glenn Yurth suggested to a grandmother that she buy a set of *The Bible Story* for each grandchild, he asked, "How many would you need?"

She quickly and readily responded, "I'd need 14 sets."

Glenn can't remember writing up the order or praying with the sister or signing her up for the Voice of Prophecy Bible course, or even telling her good-bye. He only remembers getting home to tell his wife Shirley about it.

However, he does remember very well the day he went back to deliver the books. Anything can happen when you are going back to deliver one book. And lots can happen with a whole set of books. You can have 14 times that anxiety when you are about to deliver *14 sets* of books!

Out of breath, Glenn said with his voice trembling just a bit, "Madam, I brought your books." It is good that Glenn has a strong heart, for it took some shock treatment twice in a row. She began by saying, "Mr. Yurth, I have changed my mind about the books. I have decided I need a set for myself also. Have you an extra set?"

Glenn had an extra set, so on that happy day that precious lady took 15 sets of the beautiful *Bible Story*!

When It's the Customer's Turn to Talk

After having been a literature evangelist, Milkah Wangari Wanjohi was doing some other work. One of her former customers saw her, and not knowing she had temporarily left selling books said, "Oh, friend, thank you for calling on me. Thank you for the book you sold me. You are doing a marvelous work. Please, for the people's sake, don't ever stop this work."

In relating this experience, Milkah said, "My conscience started to bother me. It was as if an angel had spoken to me, and I returned to canvassing."

Sometimes in our follow-up work we ask people, "Are the bindings holding up well? Are you using the volumes? Do you feel you paid too much for them?" We are disappointed when people say they are not using them, but very seldom do we hear them complain that they paid too much.

One man said, "I wouldn't take a thousand dollars for my book if I knew I couldn't replace it."

Another man said, "If these books would keep my children from getting into trouble, I would be willing to give up my whole farm for them."

Among the many letters in our customer file is a precious one to a literature evangelist that states, "You must be a wonderful person. I am sure the angels are looking forward to your being with them in heaven, and me too." It is not unusual for the customer to think of the literature evangelist as an angel.

Grace Huffacre and her sister at Andrews University canvassed in the summer. They said, "Our best days are rainy days. Mothers are home and they want us to read to their children."

One day a representative from the Review and Herald Publishing Association decided to do a little experimenting and see how the people were receiving our literature. He followed the steps of these girls. In one home the customer was excited over the work of these young ladies. She said, "Do you know what that little angel did? She took my child on her knee and read to her from your precious book. She was the sweetest guest I have ever had."

Customers Have Minds of Their Own

Then there is the customer who can bring the thoughtless literature evangelist back to reality. Not many people stand up and challenge the preacher who may be waxing too eloquent in the pulpit. The literature evangelist learns every day in the "college of hard knocks," however, that if he puts his star too high in the clouds the customer can bring it down.

During a Big Week I had tremendous success, a sale at every place until Wednesday. I was caught up with enthusiasm when a lady abruptly raised her hand and stopped me. "Sir," she exclaimed, "you sound as if everybody is buying these books."

I looked at her, smiled, and gave her a very foolish answer. I have been sorry for it ever since, and I paid for it that time. I should have humbly prayed a little prayer and said, "Thank you, Ma'am. I am very enthusiastic about this because of what it has done for my family and what other people say it is doing for theirs."

But I said, "I'm in a special emphasis which my organization calls Big Week, and if you don't buy you will be the first one who hasn't purchased in this entire week."

Without a smile she quickly replied, "I'll be the first one then."

The customer can also sometimes take over the selling job from the literature evangelist and do it better. In the Western Tanzania Field a very pleased customer went to his own church, gathered the people together, and showed them what he had bought. "This book, *God's Answers*, is a great volume," he told them.

A few weeks later the literature evangelist returned and learned the good news that the church wanted a copy of the book. Some time later he came again and visited the people who were members of that church. As the literature evangelist stated it, "All I had to do was deliver the books. They were already sold."

One very lovely Catholic family had nine children. The husband was a salesman himself, and they had a beautiful house. Some say it is hard to sell to salesmen, but in this case it was the salesman's wife who was cold and hard. She had every excuse why they shouldn't buy. She said, "The books are nice and I could use them in the Bible class I teach at church, but it would not be worth it. Our kids won't read them." The salesman-husband tried to convince her and I continued telling of benefits, but it seemed the more we talked the more negative she became. Finally the husband arose, went and got his check book, and wrote a check, saying, "We'll just pay cash."

Customers Are Just as Much Saints as Are Literature Evangelists

Thank God also for the loving, thoughtful customer who will pray *for the literature evangelist.* When Beverly Kinsey of

Oregon was starting her work, she was shy and afraid. She came to a home, was welcomed in by a lady, and they spent some precious moments talking about their mutual love for Jesus. The kind lady purchased *The Bible Story* and the large *Bible Readings for the Home.*

Beverly mentioned to this lady that this was her first day selling by herself and how happy she was to be treated so kindly. She signed her up for the Voice of Prophecy Bible course.

When Beverly suggested prayer, the lady quickly responded, "By all means. I would like to pray with you and for you and your new work." So they prayed together, seeking God's blessings and guidance in their lives. Can you imagine the thrill two years later when they met at the county fair at our booth display? The customer said, "You're Beverly, and I surely remember you. Tell me, are you still selling those wonderful books?"

Beverly answered that she was. Then the lady continued, "How wonderful that God has answered our prayers. You seemed so frightened that day. How often I have thought of you since that time. We have been praying for you." After chatting a bit and reassuring one another of the soon coming of the Saviour, they parted again, possibly until the kingdom.

"Her sweet prayers," Beverly says, "and the prayers of my brothers and sisters in this wonderful church continue to give me courage to face whatever God has in store for me as I do this work."

In the Philippines lives a very small man who is a literature evangelist. He is shy and at times fearful. He sold a *Great Controversy* to a big, burly man. The day he went to deliver the book the big man saw him coming and went over to the wall where he had his big knife hanging in its sheath. The little literature evangelist was sure he was going for the big machete, so he turned and ran as fast as his legs would take him. The big man took in the situation immediately and ran after him. It was quite a chase, but the little fellow realized it was a lost cause and stopped. Breathlessly the big man asked, "Aren't you the man who sells the books?"

With fear he answered, "Yes."

"You don't need to be afraid. I want my book. I keep my money in the sheath of that sword."

In western New York, one literature evangelist sold a set of *The Bible Story* and *The Great Controversy* to a family. Not long afterward they asked the literature evangelist to come to their home and study the Bible with them.

One Sabbath afternoon the literature evangelist and his family stopped to visit these people. The children of both families went down by the road to play. Soon a cry was heard. As the parents rushed to the road, they learned a child had been hit by a car. As the literature evangelist knelt beside the injured child and turned the boy over, he realized it was the son of the other family. His concern was that this tragedy might discourage the family and that they would lose faith in God and the gospel.

The little fellow was not breathing. The literature evangelist gave him mouth-to-mouth resuscitation while they waited for the ambulance. In spite of the emergency treatment the child's life ebbed away that afternoon.

In a little chapel in the hospital the literature evangelist sought to give comfort to the bereaved parents. The father said, "I'm glad we bought the books. My son enjoyed *The Bible Story* so much." Some time after this experience, this family was baptized and now rejoice in the blessed hope of the coming of Jesus when their family will be reunited.

Of any group of Christian workers the literature evangelists are usually the most enthusiastic and joyful. They are in direct contact with people. They pray in homes, sell the best Christian books and magazines in the world, leave free literature, and see people baptized.

Many Customers Recommend the Books Sold by Literature Evangelists

This letter came to us on First Baptist Church stationery:

"It is my privilege to recommend *The Bible Story, Bedtime Stories, My Bible Friends,* and *Tiny Tot Library.*

"My wife and I used *The Bible Story* and *Bedtime Stories* with our own children. All three are totally dedicated teen-age Christian young people. I not only heartily recommend these books but feel that parents do their children a great injustice by depriving them of this means of allowing the Holy Spirit to work in their young lives. There can be nothing important enough to make a parent *not able to afford them* unless a higher value is placed on material things than eternal souls.

"Very sincerely yours, ..."

Lewis Dininny received a letter from one of his customers who had purchased $400 worth of books. She wrote, "I'm enjoying my books so very much. I want you to know that I wouldn't sell them if someone offered me $5,000 for them." She meant what she said, because she purchased another $200 worth. This enthusiastic buyer concluded, "I wish I had the time to go out and tell parents everywhere how wonderful these books really are."

And last of all, when the customers are happy children, what *they* say is especially encouraging:

A boy who listened to the literature evangelist's canvass said to his dad, "I'll forget about that minibike you promised me if you'll get these books." Another one said to his dad, "I will sell my dog and help you buy the books." And other children assured their parents, "We'll go without candy, pop, and ice cream until we can get them paid for."

One mother regretted that she didn't buy the books early enough. She had listened to the canvass and decided not to buy. A few months later she phoned our literature evangelist, "Please bring those character-building books right away. I think I have waited too long; my boy got angry and kicked me this morning."

And then there were the parents who wrote to the literature evangelist, "Our little girl prayed tonight, 'Heavenly Father, please bless the man that brought us our books.'"

"You Don't Have to Be Crazy but It Helps!"

If literature evangelists couldn't laugh, this work would have ground to a halt long ago. That's why literature evangelists have a saying among themselves, "You don't have to be crazy to stay in the colporteur work, but it helps."

One literature evangelist was actually mistaken by a prospect for an escaped patient from a local mental hospital. Robert J. Wieland was going door to door when he knocked on an open door one hot day in Chattahoochee, Florida, where the Florida State Hospital for insane people was located.

As he knocked, he could see down the hallway to the kitchen. In response to his knock, a face peered around for a moment at him. Then the lady of the house came bounding down the hall to the door almost breathless. When Bob blurted out his introduction, she almost collapsed in relief. "Oh, I thought you were one of the inmates!" she said. Whenever Bob gets tempted to be proud he remembers that experience.

The Unusual Touch

Frances Fraser was one of those unusual literature evangelists who learned the message late in life. She and her physician husband had lived high socially, but after he died she was ready for the humble work of going door to door with our literature. She was serious minded, yet had a humorous streak underneath.

Naturally, she knew her way around wealthy people and knew how to meet them. Mrs. Fraser would start greeting the prospect in French, and her French greeting would catch the prospect's attention. She would explain, "In French, this expression means 'How is your liver?' You know, Mrs. so-and-so, that is very important. The condition of your liver can determine your health and even the length of your life." By this time she had her prospect's attention. Then she would introduce the health book before introducing the message books.

The literature evangelist could get discouraged if he couldn't laugh at times when he feels like crying. Henry Fitzner of Detroit met an irate lady at the door with a broom in her hand.

When Henry introduced himself and his work, she was not only brief and rude in word, but her action matched her mood. She slammed the door in his face, almost knocking him down.

It could be that she felt a little ashamed of herself, for she peeked out from behind the curtains to watch the sad look on the poor literature evangelist's face. Henry walked quickly out to the sidewalk, and then looked back at the door and began to laugh.

Soon the lady yanked the door open and demanded, "Man, what are you laughing at?"

Henry smiled politely, and said, "Madam, I was just thinking how good it was that you didn't hit me with that broom!"

For some seconds there was only silence. Somehow it tickled her and she began to laugh too. She finally said, "I'm sorry. Come in and explain your visit." She ended up buying his book.

The Angels Must Laugh Too

Sometimes the joke is not on the literature evangelist but on the other person involved. Down in the beautiful Spanish lands a young literature evangelist was getting more and more nervous on his book delivery day because his roll of money was getting larger and larger.

Sure enough, a hoodlum had been watching him and knew of his delivery day.

When the attack came, the literature evangelist was afraid for his life, but all the robber demanded was, "Give me the money!"

When our literature evangelist gave him the roll of money, the bandit, confident that he had it all, stuffed it down deep in his pocket. As he was about ready to take flight, he got another idea. He would be a lot harder to detect if he was wearing somebody else's clothes. So he turned and demanded, "Your suit's very nice. Give me that, too."

Our literature evangelist gave him his clothes, which he quickly jumped into. Soon he was on his way, leaving his dirty rags.

With a broken heart the literature evangelist slipped into those old rags and started on his weary way. As he was feeling so sorry for himself, he stuck his hands down in the ragged old pockets. His eyes brightened and his step quickened, for his hand touched a big wad of paper. It was his roll of money! Now he was jubilant, praising the Lord. The robber had left the literature evangelist's big roll of money in the pocket of the worn suit of clothes!

Literature Evangelists' Prayers Are Special

One literature evangelist was very surprised one day when a man met him at the door, held out his hands, and said, "Where are my books? Come on in." The literature evangelist was shocked, but he had prayed for the Lord's guidance and blessing. The customer was anxious to explain, "I had a dream that a man would come and bring me some books."

The literature evangelist brought out *The Great Controversy* and *The Desire of Ages*. As soon as the man saw the covers, he cried, "These are my books. These are the very books I saw in my dream, Bless you! *God* sent you."

Day by day, faithful literature evangelists around the world beg the Lord to prepare the way before them. Marius Pelser, while canvassing just outside Johannesburg, South Africa, one morning received a distinct impression: "Go to the end house on the street." He drove up to this house and met Mr. Oosthuizen, who was sitting in a wheelchair. He and his wife were very friendly and told him the following story: "More than four years ago I heard the message of the Seventh-day Adventist Church. I was convinced it was God's true message, but I resisted and tried to forget it.

"Several months later I became paralyzed and have been confined to this wheelchair ever since. I've visited the best of doctors and faith healers from different churches, but all in vain."

Marius then told them about his distinct impression to visit them. He encouraged them to put their full trust in the Lord, and bowing their heads together he prayed a simple but earnest prayer. Minutes later, before his astonished wife, Mr. Oosthuizen got up out of his wheelchair and walked normally for the first time in four years! They are now enjoying our literature and receiving Bible studies before joining the church. The news of this healing has caused other families in the area who were previously prejudiced to accept our books into their homes.

"I'll Tear Your Briefcase to Pieces"

A student literature evangelist in Korea was sitting on the floor, according to custom, across from his prospect, presenting the book, *The Desire of Ages.*

The kindhearted prospect was interested in the book. He called to his wife in their little kitchen, "Yobo, bring me the money." But the big teenage son came into the room, storming, yelling, "You, evil one, get out of this house. We're not buying that book." He walked up as if he were demon-possessed. The literature evangelist was still sitting on the floor. The maddened youth grabbed him by the throat and started to choke him, exclaiming in wild fury, "I will break your neck!"

He released his grip and stood back. There was total silence. The mother said nothing. The literature evangelist said nothing, except to send up another silent prayer for help. Then the youth grabbed the literature evangelist's briefcase, screaming, "I'll tear your briefcase to pieces!" Again the literature evangelist prayed. And almost as suddenly as the young man entered the room, he marched out again, mumbling to himself as though he were being physically taken away.

Still surprisingly calm, the father and owner of the house said to his wife, "Bring me the money." He quickly paid for his book.

The man read his book, accepted it readily, and soon became a baptized member of the church. Immediately he tried to convince his family. Much to the surprise of everyone, the young man who had put on such a scene was able to see the message also. He applied to attend our college, where he began studying for the ministry.

When I was at the college, recruiting students to go out canvassing during the holidays, he applied. I had the privilege of canvassing with him the day he told me this interesting story. Today he is one of our pastors and his father is a local church elder.

"Seize That Man's Case"

"When I entered the courthouse," says a humble literature evangelist in Central Africa, "I went first to the highest officer, the judge himself. 'Send me an officer,' he barked, and banged the receiver down.

"A security officer stepped in, saluted, and awaited his order. The judge snapped, 'Seize that man's case. I know who you people are. You come in here making trouble. I'm tired of it.' Then he went on with his work at the desk.

"There was nothing I could do. With no books to show, I had nothing to say, so I left. The guard at the door asked me, 'Where is your case?' I told him they had taken my case away from me. He nodded. I left, and went straight home.

"I did not eat supper. I went to my bed and knelt down to pray. I prayed all night. I did not eat breakfast either, but went right back to the courthouse. I was permitted by the guard to enter and went to the office of the judge.

"Now I don't know why I did what I did, but I walked straight up to his desk, dropped to my knees, and started to pray out loud, "Oh God, You have chosen this man to be our judge. Help him to judge rightly. Bless this man. We know you appointed him. . . .' I don't remember what else I prayed for in that short prayer, but I prayed in the name of Jesus. I got up and said, 'Judge, I am sorry for the misunderstanding of yesterday. I thought I would come today and explain what I do.'

"Without a word the judge picked up the phone and called security. 'Bring that briefcase back to my office.' When he handed it to me, I showed him every book in the case and told him the benefits of these books to the people and to his community. Whereupon the judge, touched by the Spirit of God, bought every book I had in the case. The day before, I went in with a heavy briefcase and out with no briefcase and a heavy heart. But today I went out with a light briefcase, a light heart, and a heavy pocket full of money!"

God Speaks to Three-Year-Old Jeff

Paul Cordray was experiencing what many literature evangelists do at one time or another—a sales slump. Day after day his little three-year-old son Jeff heard his mother and daddy pleading with the Lord for success. Of course, Paul's wife, Judy, prayed at other times, too, and little Jeff felt the anxiety.

Day after day Paul went to his work but came home in the evening without sales. One evening while Daddy was out working, Jeff awakened, got out of bed, and ran to his mother, saying, "We must pray for Daddy!" So they did. Jeff went back to bed and slept soundly, knowing their prayers had been answered.

When Paul got home, Judy met him at the door and exclaimed, "You had success tonight!"

Paul asked, "How did you know?"

Then she related how Jesus had awakened and impressed little Jeff, and how confident Jeff was that the angels would help his daddy.

Jeff's prayer was little, but here is how a literature evangelist's big prayer found a ready answer in less that 24 hours. Sandy Dancek, a Pennsylvania literature evangelist, tells this happy experience:

"One Sabbath I was talking to a lady about sending her grandson to church school. She and her husband were retired and could not afford the added expense, though they really wanted him to go. I told her that her desire to have her grandson receive a Christian education was enough; God would provide the money. And I prayed with them.

"The very next day, Sunday, my son Eddie and I canvassed together. We called on a lady who works night shifts and whom I had not been able to find at home on weekdays. After looking at the books, she said, 'You are Adventists, aren't you?' We said we surely were. Then she told us, 'I used to be an Adventist—even a literature evangelist. My husband died and now I'm married to a Catholic and have not attended church in years.

"'You probably won't believe this,' she continued, 'but I have been praying that God would send someone to my home to tell me where to donate some money.' I told her about the young boy who wanted to go to church school and about his need for tuition. 'You have it,' she said. 'Years ago when my children were little I was too poor to pay their tuition, and other church members paid their whole way through. I have been praying that I could help someone else.'

"Eddie and I were dumfounded! I knew God would provide this boy's tuition, but I didn't expect an answer so soon, and then from a stranger. She also bought *The Bible Story* and *Bedtime Stories* for her own grandchildren."

When a Literature Evangelist Is Almost a Prophet

Sometimes a literature evangelist is moved by the Holy Spirit to say something very bold. One evening after a busy day of work, a young lady literature evangelist who canvasses in the mountains and villages of Mindanao, Philippines, was looking for a place to stay overnight. Houses were few.

In the distance she saw a government military post. She approached the gate and asked the soldier in charge if there was a place where she could sleep that night. He was polite but to the point, "Absolutely not!" Word had been received that rebels intended to destroy this camp that very night. She made the same request to the officer in charge and he gave a similar reply. She responded by saying, "Sir, if you permit me to stay here overnight, I promise you the rebels will not come."

"How can you guarantee such a thing?" he asked.

"Because I am a literature evangelist, a Christian worker for God; and wherever I go, a special angel goes with me." She was granted a place to stay!

The next morning officers and soldiers lined up in front of the gate to say Thank You and Farewell to the heavenly messenger. Not a shot had been fired through the night, a most unusual thing for that mountain outpost.

A very precious widow wanted to purchase a fifteen-dollar Bible book, but she had only five dollars. She said, "I will pray and God will help me get the balance."

When the literature evangelist went back to her home, the lady came from her garden behind her house and, reaching into her pocket, pulled out a ten-dollar bill. She said, "Before I give you this money, I want to tell you a story. I knew you were coming today, Monday. Saturday evening I still didn't have the money, but I was sure that the Lord wouldn't let a poor widow down. I was praying when a knock came on the door. I went down and there stood a man for whom I had worked some time before.

"He said, 'I didn't know until recently that your husband had died. For three nights now I have not been able to sleep thinking that I didn't pay you enough when you worked for me. Here is ten dollars. I want to get back to sleep!'"

And so, day by day around the world, the play and interplay of heavenly agencies continues behind the scenes in answer to the prayers of dedicated literature evangelists.

What Keeps Us Going Until the Lord Returns

Two brothers, Simon and James, were living in Mbarara, Uganda. Simon always listened to his mother, who taught her children the Word of God from the time they were young.

When they were older, the boys moved to town. James forgot his mother's God and acquired bad habits. However, Simon cherished the teaching of his mother. One day Simon bought *The Desire of Ages* from a literature evangelist. As he read it, his spiritual commitment strengthened.

James joined a gang who lived by robbing houses, businesses, and banks. Simon tried to talk some sense into James by showing him where this life would lead. But James refused to listen.

One night James and his gang broke into a house and killed a man and his son. Immediately the police were alerted. James ran home and awakened his brother. When Simon turned on the light he found James' clothes covered with blood. Wide-eyed with fear, James begged Simon to help him. Suddenly Simon ordered, "James, take off your stained clothes and put on mine." Simon himself put on the blood-stained ones. Shortly the police dashed into the room, arrested Simon and put him in prison.

In prison Simon wrote to James, asking him to read *The Desire of Ages*, which he had left behind. By reading this book and the Bible, James was converted. He decided to go and trade places with his brother, and die for his own crime. Unfortunately the judge could not be convinced that Simon was not the murderer. So the sentence held that was passed on Simon.

Finally the day of Simon's death came, but he was not afraid, for he knew he was innocent and his heart was right with God. Before Simon died, he wrote a simple letter to James, stating, "I am going to die for your crime, James. I pray you will become like Jesus, an heir of salvation."

One wonders if anyone around the world has been so motivated by reading *The Desire of Ages*! But there are indeed many who do respond to the grand Original of such self-sacrificing love, and who devote their lives to proclaiming it.

In Tanzania, East Africa, a literature evangelist was having such good success selling our books that the evil one was stirred up. Someone without any provocation accused him of stealing, and yelled, "Thief! Thief!" That cry always electrifies an African crowd.

In the great confusion emotions ran high. One person called out, "Who gave you permission to sell here?" Women and children gathered with clubs as they do to kill a thief or drive someone out of town.

It may have been an evil angel in the form of a man who screamed, "Let's finish him." The literature evangelist stood quietly and prayed, "I will die. Lord, you brought me here. Please remember that I have four children. I want to see them in heaven."

The mob started chanting a devilish, "Let's finish him! Let's finish him!"

When the ones nearest him tried to bring their clubs down on his head, they found they could raise their clubs but something stayed their hands so they could not bring them down. Someone called, "Take him to the police."

They started off, half pulling him to the police station. The police were surprised that the mob would bring a man in like this instead of taking the law into their own hands. "What's going on?" they asked.

"This man came to force the people to buy books," several said.

The police calmed them, stating, "Let's be reasonable. Untie him so we can hear him."

They had carried his briefcase along. Now his hands were free, the briefcase was near, so he gave the police a sales talk, introducing his books.

"How much are they?" the police questioned.

"Only 95 shillings," the literature evangelist answered.

Then the policeman said, "Write your receipt and give me one. I would like to have that book." The people were astonished.

Another policeman bought a book and another asked, "Have you got a Bible?"

One by one the people slipped away who had brought him in. The literature evangelist sold 800 shillings' worth there in a few minutes and signed up seven for the Voice of Prophecy Bible course. Then the police said to him, "Please excuse the people for the way they have treated you."

"Oh, that's OK," the literature evangelist replied. "They brought me here to work."

Many literature evangelists devote their entire lifetime to a labor of love of visiting people in their homes. And they have been successful in supporting their families throughout their careers. One of them is Charles Eddy. He had been highly successful in other sales fields, and he became a literature evangelist in 1952 with a determination to succeed. His sales records were phenomenal.

During these decades, his wife, Helen, and their three children shared Charles' dedication and loyalty, willingly making the sacrifices that were essential for his success.

Often Charles would have to leave home Monday mornings and not return until Friday. No word of complaint was ever heard from his family. They have stood solidly together during 26 years in the literature ministry and have had the joy of seeing 120 of their customers baptized.

Naturally, Charles' success impressed publishing leaders to invite him into leadership and administrative roles, but he returned to his first love, door-to-door ministry. When Charles finished college, he accepted God's call: "If there is one work more important than another, it is that of getting our publications before the public" (*Colporteur Ministry*, p. 7). Brother Eddy never turned aside from what he believed was a call from the Lord, and the Lord never turned aside from blessing and honoring His servant.

And so, in sunshine and shadow, in laughter and in tears, the army of literature evangelists follow where Jesus leads them, confident of His never-failing fellowship.

Wouldn't you like to take your place in this grand work?